Doug

Tales of the Barbershop

Reviews

This book is almost unbelievable ... Hairy Clipping

It made the hair on the back of me Neck stand on end ... William Wallace

Most Chairs occupied in Winfield ... Mayhor Turnover

Would like a second read with donuts ... Joey Brown

The last story was a close shave ... Popeye

Also by Doug Ehorn

Keeneyville Kids

Keeneyville Kids 2

Kissed by the Sun

Doug Tales

The Brownstone

The Brownstone: The Beginning

The Brownstone: The Gathering

The Brownstone: Adventures of the Mind

The Brownstone: Anna Journey

The Brownstone: Flights of Fantasy

The Brownstone: The Key

Poems: From the Heart

Poems: Songs of the Heart

Targhee's Mountain Man

The Eddie Chronicles

Code Word: Frond Calamity

Changing Chaos

Leftovers: A Collection of Stories

My First 100 Years

Tales of the Barber Shop

West of Time

The Last Call

Willie's Cafe

Smiley Jack

Sampler

Poems of Tomorrow

Harrison Lane

Josh Knoland: Confrontations

Poems of Tomorrow

Harrison Lane

Poems: Escaping Reality

Portals to Another Time

Youthful Remembrances
-With Anita Huckins

Doug Ehorn

Tales of the Barbershop

A Book of Short Stories by
Doug Ehorn

This book is a work of fiction. Names, characters, places, and incidents herein are either products of the author's imagination or are used fictitiously. Any resemblance to actual places, incidents, or people, living or dead, is entirely coincidental.

Copyright © 2015 by Doug Ehorn
All Rights Reserved.

Lest We Forget Publications, LLC

Written at Casa Blanca, COTU

This is the authorized First Edition

ISBN-13: 9781-1508-8607-1
ISBN-10: 1-5088-6047-1

6.01.2015 start

The New Book

To

Robin and her co-workers at
Sportsman Barber Shop

Robin
Gina
Vicki
Robin
Jacki

Jewell Road
Winfield, Illinois 60190

The New Book

Table of Contents

What is Barbering
Tales of the Barbershop
The Barbershop
The Giant TV
Concerns of a Third Grader
The Winter of Our Malcontent
A Slow Day
Beaufort, South Carolina
Holding Down the Shop
County Fair Week
Cucumber Salad
Equality
Skunked
Rascal at the Barbershop
Cantigny
Retirement: A Perspective
How the World Works
Farmers' Market
In Between Holidays
Winfield Veterans
The Adoption
Cytoplasm
Checkers at the Shop
Broken Water
The Not So Silent Shop
Moving Heads About
Cantigny Revisited
The Garden
Billie
 A Close Shave

The New Book

Tales of the Barbershop

Judges 16:17

INTRODUCTION TO THE TOPIC

What is the history of barbering?

Have you ever wondered where the word 'barber' originated? The term comes from the word 'barba', which means beard. In ancient Egyptian and Asian civilizations, it was believed that both good and evil spirits entered people through the hairs on their heads and their faces. Thus, barbers were highly revered and respected. The belief at the time was that the only way to rid people of the evil spirits invading their bodies was to cut their hair.

Barbers were so idolized at this time that they were allowed to routinely perform religious and marriage ceremonies. In preparation for marriage, both bride and groom were encouraged to grow their hair long and then shake out evil spirits at a dance after the ceremony. After marriage, the barber would cut the hair short in order to keep evil spirits at bay.

Why do barber shops display a red and white barber pole?

In ancient times, barbers performed many duties in addition to cutting hair. They were also expected to act as surgeons, dentists and religious officials. The red and white pole that you see outside of many barber shops today is in reference to a time when barbers were expected to engage in bloodletting in order to heal people. The ribbons represent two bandages, with one being red for the color of blood and the other being white to represent the color of the bandage to stop the bleeding.

The first barber organization was formed in Rome around the year 1094. At that time, barbers were referred to as barber surgeons, because they also performed teeth extraction, cupping and leeching, bloodletting, surgery and enemas. Some of the more modern barber practices, such as shaving, hair cutting and hair styling, were also performed. The occasion of an adolescent boy's first shave was seen as a major rite of passage in ancient societies, so it was not uncommon for a celebration to take place at the barber shop during the shaving.

Today's barber shop bears little resemblance to barber shops of times gone by. For one thing, a barber is not expected to play the role of other medical professions at the same time. Barbers are free to focus on meeting only the cosmetic needs of their customers. Beginning around the early 1900s, barber shops became a place for men to socialize and hear the daily news and gossip. Most barber shops were owned by tradesmen who set up their shops in storefronts of small towns.

How did modern-day barbering come about?

In 1893, the first barber college opened in Chicago, Illinois, followed by two more barber colleges in Iowa in 1899 and 1900. Over the course of the next 20 years, barbers began to be recognized as professionals who could trim men's hair and treat disorders of the skin and scalp. The profession was dominated by men until approximately 1980. At that time, a shift had occurred and almost half of all barber school graduates were women. That trend continues today, and nearly half the barbering work force is women.

Considering a career in barbering?

It's a great place to chew the fat with other men.

When I went to hair stylists, I hardly ever talked to the woman who cut my hair. I'd chat about my family and theirs and that's about it. The woman who cut my hair usually ended up chatting with the other women in the salon, while I sat there awkwardly.

Barbers, on the other hand, are interesting people with interesting stories to tell. On my visits to the barber shop, I've met a retired Army Ranger colonel, a musician who spent 13 years on the road in a jazz band, and a man who is the third generation in his family to take up the profession. Each of them had fascinating stories to share. And I in turn feel at ease to say what's on my mind. There is conversation about politics, cars, sports, and family. Guys read the newspaper and comment on current events. In between the banter, jokes are told and laughs are had. And *everyone* is involved: the barbers, the customers getting their haircut, and the customers waiting to get their haircut. Adding to the enjoyment is that a variety of men take part in the conversation; young, old, and middle-aged join in the mix.

I think there's a good argument that barbershops are among America's last civic forums. Where do people go today just to talk with others in the community? Coffee shops? Every time I go to a coffee shop, people are at their own tables minding their own business. The only other place that I can think of is a bar, but bars are now co-ed instead of being bastions of manliness. Graduate student, Melissa Harris-Lacewell, wrote an article about how discussions in traditionally black barbershops shape political ideas in the African-American community. She noted how political debate in barbershops can be vigorous and engages young and old alike. Unfortunately, white Americans are missing out on this experience. So, if you're wanting to get your thumb on the pulse of civic life in your community, head over to the barbershop.

You can get a great shave.

Many barbershops still give traditional single blade razor shaves. You haven't lived until you've experienced the pleasures of a great shave at a barber. This past weekend, I went to a barber here in town to get a shave. I reclined in the plush old school barber chairs that had ash trays in the arm rests, a throwback to a time when people could smoke in public places. Then my shave commenced. The barber first wrapped a hot towel around my face. Next, the barber massaged in a lemon based cream to clean out my pores.

After that, several more hot towels were applied. By then, I was feeling nice and relaxed, on the verge of falling asleep relaxed. The barber then massaged in some cocoa butter to soften my beard. Next, the barber brushed a warm lather into my beard that smelled like 'man' and not like that crappy artificial goo you buy in a can. The barber then took a piece of razor sharp metal and scraped my beard off for the closest, best shave I've ever had. Allowing another man to hold a razor to your neck is a good way to remind yourself that you're alive.

To finish it all off, I got another hot towel wrapped on my face along with a final face massage with a soothing vanishing cream. When I stepped out of the shop, I felt like a new man, ready to take on the world.

It's a great activity to do with your father or son.

Men need traditions that can help bond them together. Visiting the barbershop with your father or son is a great tradition to begin in your family. Many men have been going to the same barber all their life and have introduced their sons to the same chair and the same barber. What a great way to bond with the men in your life!

You'll feel manlier.

Every time I go to the barber shop I just feel manlier. I don't know what it is. Perhaps it's the combination of the smell of hair tonics and the all-man atmosphere. But more so, it's the awareness of the tradition of barbershops. Barbershops are places of continuity; they don't change with the shifts in culture. The places and barbers look the same as they did when your dad got his hair cut. It's a straightforward experience with none of the foofoo accouterments of the modern age. There are no waxings, facials, highlights, or appointments. Just great haircuts and great conversation.

When you walk out of the barber shop with a sharp haircut, you can't help but feel a bit of manly swagger creep into your step. So next time you spot that familiar red and white striped pole, stop in. You'll be glad you did.

You can even feel manly if you let a woman cut your hair!

Most of the above material was borrowed from files on the internet.

The New Book

The New Book

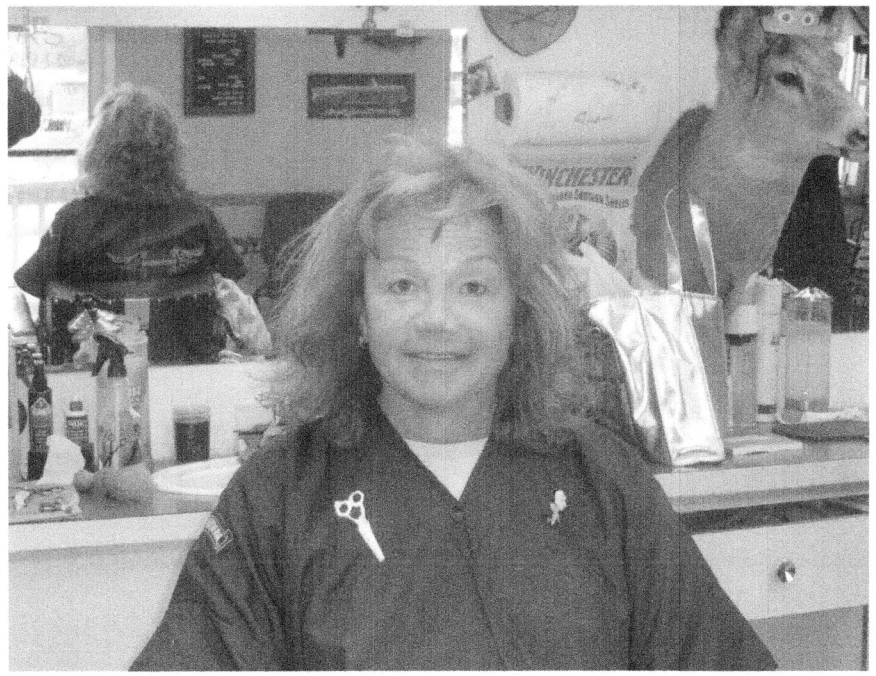

Chapter 1

Tales from the Barbershop

The barbershop in town is a place where you go to swap stories and get a haircut. You may not even know that the driving force to go there is really so you can share a story with the barber. But it is and you talk about almost anything as if one of the gals at the shop in your best friend. Well, just maybe she is!

On any given day from 10 AM to 5:30 PM you might go and sit in a chair and wait your turn. You can be one of those in the lively conversation that happens while people are getting their haircut, or you can just sit and listen or ignore. The option is yours. I think that you will learn that even if the barber and the person sitting in the chair are talking too loud, they don't want you to interrupt them during their talking time. You get your own when you are ready to pay for your time.

There are always exceptions to that, especially if you know the guy getting the cut. Good old friends are allowed to enter the conversation, but others like me, who rarely go to the shop, are not allowed to butt in as it may be. So most of the time, I try to hide behind a newspaper or a magazine acting like I am reading. The truth is that I forgot my reading glasses so I cannot read very much after the headlines and other similar things with big print. So I have to sit still and mind my own business.

But what if you just sat and listened quietly and took a few notes while no one was looking. There are a lot of human interest stories floating around. There is no telling who might come up with the best zinger of the day. It could be the barber lady herself.

Human interest stories coming rolling out of most people's minds while in the chair. They just get started when the barber lady trying to increase her tip begins a simple discussion about your day. If you had a bad one, she talks you into a good afternoon. And the best part of this whole experience, I have never met a barber who had a bad day. All of their days are the second or third best that ever happened in the whole world. Just ask them.

Human nature or condition being what it is is ready to spill a tale or two. Sometimes the tale is short and you have to ready between the lines. Barber ladies are good at sorting out the story bits and feeding it back to you so you continue on until your day improves.

Just think about it, you can get $250 of therapy for only a $15.00 flat rate! That is the best bargain in town. And you get the back of your neck cleaned off, too!

It is no wonder why men go to the barbershop in town. The four ladies are waiting for the men to parade in. They seem to know half of the men by name; a few by reputation; and a couple others by face. I am one of the face people I am sure. But I get a nice treatment each time and I am thankful for the therapy session.

But today, I was at the shop and it occurred to me that I just might have an opportunity to glean some stories for a book about happenings around town. If I keep the peoples' names out of the stories and fib a little, I just might get away with spinning a tale or two.

Since Floyd the Barber is not available and giving out advice to Andy Taylor and Deputy Fife, I am more that pleased to present Winfield's version of our home town one haircut at a time.

Perhaps your story will be next. See ya there if you are willing.

Now on to the first story.

Chapter 2

The Barbershop

Everything has a beginning and soon I was wondering about how this gaggle of five ladies got together and became the iconic barbershop in town. When I first moved into the town twenty some years ago I am sure I got my hair cut at this building. At the time it was owned by a man who was either getting up in age or in grumpiness. At any rate he had reached a point where he knew it was time to cash out.

To tell the truth, I have no real idea when this occurred. I don't want to spill too many beans and ask the ladies how long they worked there and how one of them came to own the shop. There are some PC rules that one must abide and I am not going to try to tear down any walls just to satisfy my own curiosity. I am not made of such material. I can go for days on end not asking a single question. My wife will testify to that as each day she asks me what someone said or did. I have no real clue to current things. My mind is about 1950 and 1960 as they say 24/7.

Well back to the barbershop for a while before I get distracted again.

The white building located on Jewell Road (aka Jewel Road) is on the north side of the street and across from the parking lot from the train station. There is a parking lot in the back of the building to accommodate hair cut traffic. That lot is coupled with the three space along the road in front and make it easy enough to find a place to park and gage the amount of time you might have to spend waiting. I have driven by and viewed the street spaces full and saw a few cars in the back. That just tells me to go on with my activities and come back later. The girls will tell you I don't return too often. When I sit in the chair, I "NEED" a haircut.

One thing that confuses me about the building is that there is a hair salon at the east end of the building and it does not seem to be occupied. To me that is a missed opportunity for someone. The area could be turned into a standup bar, a game room or a popcorn shop that would attract people waiting for haircuts. Then Robin could install one of those 'Take a Number' things and you could go do some activity until you were paged. Now if she takes up this advice, I want 15% of the profits.

The interior of the barber shop meets the standards of what you might think a barber shop with the name "Sportsmans" might have. There are seven heads of animals on the walls include a Bison, deer, a boar and a few antelope. Then there are other relics; some are real and some are surreal at best. Pictures and jerseys fill in the rest of the wall covering saving Robin a lot of cash that might be spent on paint. That is just the way a man likes his surroundings as he is clipped.

Robin will tell you that when she bought the place, several deer heads were there. There were other things that seemed to fall apart over the years and ended up in the trash. Probably a good thing. So she welcomed new materials including that pheasant with its wings partially opened. In the years I have gone there I have not noticed a lot of change in the décor, it is manly in this little world of five lady barbers. Ironic, ain't it?

Well, if you move down the line in the four chairs you get little bits of information about the ladies. I was amazed to find that they all attended the same barber school in Aurora with three of the five graduating in the same class. One of the ladies was a little behind at school but somehow was friends with the trio and at a time when she could join, the gang took her in.

Seems that this one had a really bad boss on her first job. He was cranky and all that and it was drudgery going in to cut hair. But that all changed as she was accepted into the little Center of the Universe clique. Now the happy fivesome seems totally compatible, at least in front of us payers, and go about their business in a dignified way. The only ups and downs in this shop are the elevation of the chairs as they are alternately pumped up or release to allow a person to reach back to Mother Earth at the end of a cut.

I am not one who has any particular favorite barber in the shop. Some seem to have a favorite barber and will wait a couple of extra minutes to get their favorite lady. Perhaps that is because of the discussions the two might have as the hair cut proceeds. You get to a level of comfort in the discussions, and just maybe in the hair cut, too. The lady will ask how Aunt Bertha is doing and if the kid was still playing the piano. These bits of detail can turn into long term relationships. So much so that when the lady goes on vacation, the man does too since he does not want his hair cut by the others.

Thank goodness for those who have favorites and those who don't.

I personally think that the diversity of the discussions is good and moving from chair to chair is welcome. In many ways this astute group knows who most of the clients are and can pull up a few details about the family. Now that makes one feel at home. One day perhaps Robin will ask all of the clients to Thanksgiving Dinner. Who knows?

Nothing happens in town that does not get aired in the barber shop. If you can hear the stories fly around the place you would have enough information to run for mayor. But the televisions and the cacophony of the interior seems to deliberately impede a full hearing or understanding. Maybe on my part it is just old age setting in. It could be the three conversations going on in my head.

On a wintery day with the sun blasting through the plate glass window facing south, the room is warm and the atmosphere light and happy. A train rumbles through town and you know all is well. Then you hear the magic word.

"Next."

Chapter **3**

The Giant TV

There is always a way to do something if you have the will, the imagination and the spirit to get around the rules. Jeff and Tom decided that between themselves that had all of those qualities and they were determined to show that the impossible can be completed even if you had to weasel your way into the final end. People can be duped you know. Well, maybe not all of the time. What is it that Abraham Lincoln said?

"You can fool some of the people all of the time and all of the people some of the time …."

Jeff didn't know that line at the time, but in the next two weeks he sure would.

It all started out one day when Jeff and Tom thought it would be a good idea to have a color television in their bedroom. That way they could watch TV choices of their own and play video games on the giant screen until their fingers hurt so bad that they might have to go to the hospital for some medicine. On a rainy day when nothing was really happening, Jeff told Tom that they should go ask mom if she would buy a TV for their room. They set down at the desk and wrote out five reasons why this was a good idea.

1. It would be a way to stay out of trouble;

2. Mom would not have to fight to watch her shows;

3. Other boys in their class had one;

4. It would be less noisy in the front room;

5. It would help them do their homework.

Now everyone of those reason sounded good to the two boys and they practiced saying the lines in front of a mirror so that they would not laugh at any of the lines. This had to look like a serious presentation. Who knows if the opportunity would every come again. Now it was going to come down to the correct timing.

Moms are not too good at listening if they are trying to cook, talking to their friends on the phone or paying the bills. Well maybe that last one could be an advantage in some cases when you needed a quick answer or just an excuse you could use later when mom would ask what got into you.

"Well, mom, you did approve it, dontcha remember?"

Ever wonder how many times you could use that excuse? Jeff did and one month he tried it about six times. Finally, mom just set down the phone and said, "NO. NO to anything you just asked. The answer is NO. Got it? Now leave me alone for two minutes."

Well that would seem to settle that one question. But there would come another chance in a day or two and if you were ready and had on your best running shoes you might get a nod that really meant "Wait a second" and you would use that as the exit strategy. Off on the way you would go and not look back. It helped if the bike you owned was in the right position at the doorway. Around the corner you would go before mom could get to the door.

The New Book

Now the next part of the strategy would be – stay away long enough so that when you got home mom would be making supper. Rush in and shout, "I gotta go upstairs and wash up, mom. Whatever you are cooking smells good!"

Being gratified that she was appreciated, she would settle down and finish her tasks. Then you would stay upstairs and pretend to do your homework. Emphasis on pretend.

Well, one day came when mom and dad were going on a short vacation that they had planned for some time. Uncle Billy was going to stay with the boys. He was a lot of fun to have around and he loved to play video games. So the best thing to do was when you came into a room just hit the button and go to the television and interrupt his game. This would soften him up. He would let you do it a time or two, but soon he would have enough. So you work him over a few months in advance so he knows that he will never get the game completed. Then you watch for him to be winning a game with a very high score and come in and politely ask if he might take you to Best Buy so you can get a few things. He will think video games and he was all for you spending money on things he could use.

"Let me put this game on pause and we can go if you are ready."

"Oh, yeah," came the twin voices. There was a lot of excitement in the air.

On the way to Best Buy, Uncle Billy was dreaming about the new 'Rover 3 Game' that had come out last week. If you were going to buy it he would be able to play it all night after he got you in bed. He was hinting around to see what you had in mind, but you would talk to your brother and let Billy just stew during the ride. He needed to get past a certain point so he would not turn around.

For three months Jeff and Tom had been saving up birthday gifts. Each time one of the relatives asked what you wanted for a present the boys asked for a gift card from Best Buy. Then on a future day the boys could get the most up to date games or some other joy. The joint kitty was well over four hundred dollars. So if the advertisement from Best Buy was right a 36 inch color TV was in range. That would fit very nicely on the desk.

So Billy was conned in taking the two boys to Best Buy under false assumptions. He would later have to plead innocent to his sister.

Entering the story the boys disappeared immediately. Billy thought he would catch up with them in the games section so he had little worry about them running ahead. "Let them get some of that energy out of themselves. That might give me more time on the games."

So Billy wandered past a number of electronic deals and stopped to play with an item or two. The new classy phones could do almost anything but dig a ditch. So he asked the guy behind the counter to show him a few of the aps. Twenty minutes flew by before Billy took notice that he was supposed to be with the boys. What might they be up to? Time to go check.

Seeing no one he knew in the games area, he began the search through the store for his charges. A bit of a panic was setting in. The first six aisles were not producing the desired results. Where could those boys be? He went over to the Television section of the store. Not a single person under thirty there.

"Can I help you?" the courteous man said to Billy.

"Well, not really. I am not going to buy a TV. But have you seen two eleven year old boys running around here?"

The New Book

"Do you mean Jeff and Tom?"

"Yeah that would be them."

"They are up at the checkout counter right now. I took them up there a few minutes ago."

Billy made a beeline to the front of the store. There he saw Jeff at the counter and Tom was nearby looking at a few items. He doubled his pace to get up there.

"What are you up to?"

"We are buying a new TV for our room. Mom and dad said that we could get it while they were gone. I thought I told you that was why we were coming here," said Jeff.

"Ah I don't know if that is a good idea. Why wouldn't your dad come with you before he left?"

"Well, you know how much time he works and how he gets so busy he doesn't have time to even pack his suitcase. That is why he left you that note on the table."

"Well, alright. How are you paying for this?"

"We have enough money in gift cards from our birthdays and other times. So mom said we could use the cards."

The transaction was finished and Jeff moved to the front of the store. "Can you get the car up here so we can load this monster?"

Billy looked at Jeff and still had some doubts about this whole thing. But the TV was now paid for and it was time to move on. He went and brought the car to the front of the store. The box slid into the back part of the SUV with very little trouble. Soon Billy was heading for home. The vision of Rover 3 seemed to have crashed in his mind. The new TV was front and center and perhaps that was a good deal. No longer would the boys upset his game playing while he stayed with them. That made the trip to the store worthwhile.

All three of this group lifted and carried the box into the house. It was not that heavy, but the box was huge and clumsy. The box was carefully opened and the TV extracted. Up the stairs it went quickly and on top of the desk it found its resting place.

"Should I help you set it up?" said Billy.

"Naw! I am sure we can handle it from here."

The box was taken out of the house and put along the recycle bin. In two days it would be hauled away. Mom and dad came home in one day! Jeff and Tom did not think that part out.

For a whole day they never seemed to leave their room. TV and games were going at least 20 hours that first day. The second day there would be more time. The boys were working the games in shifts at times. One boy would rest and the other played. When both felt the urge, they played games against each other. Then they got Billy involved. Billy was downstairs and the boys upstairs as they play 'Tiger Man V. 6'. That was about the coolest game out these days, except Rover 3.

Mom and dad pulled in the drive way and immediately saw the box. They stopped on their way in and noted the printing on the box - 36 inch TV.

"Billy!"

The sound of his sister's voice told a volume. He snuck out the front door and was gone. How did he let the boys get away with this? He would pay dearly if Karen ever caught up with him.

The End

Chapter 4

Concerns of a Third Grader

The young man sat tall in the chair and was still for a few minutes. Robin started by spraying the lad's hair with water and running a comb through his hair. The boy wiggled his face as some droplets settled on his face. His nose twitched. Now the actual cutting process would begin. Robin used her hands to gather up parts of the hair and cut it to a uniform length. This went on for a few minutes while Josh sat still. The conversation began with Robin telling the boy that one day last week a dead mouse was found in the barber shop. This got the boy's attention alright!

Immediately you could tell that Robin's success was related to how she could draw out a conversation with almost anyone. The boy quietly started to talk with her.

"The mouse was right here by this chair!" the barber said as she pointed to the floor by the side of the chair. She pointed downward with her scissors to make her point.

"Right here?"

"Yes. It was dead and not moving one little bit."

"Did the guts hang out of it?"

That statement would have caught many off guard, but now the time spent working with kids became obvious. Robin just gave a quick laugh and continued on keeping the conversation fresh and alive.

"No, it was freshly dead and it was still kind of wiggly. But dead for a while. No guts"

"That's too bad. I would have liked it if the guts were hanging out and making the floor a bit messy. I could imagine showing it to my friends and then to my sister. I don't think she would have liked it very much."

"I think I can understand that," said Robin. She was trying not to laugh so that the boy would continue to discuss the mouse.

"So what did you do with the mouse?"

Robin paused from cutting the lad's hair and stood with her hands on her hips. She looked at Josh and said, "I didn't want to pick it up myself. I don't like mice very much. One of the men who came in to get a haircut told me he would pick it up."

"Oh good! Was he going to give it to you or take it home?"

"No, I asked him to throw it away."

"Well, where did he throw it?" The boy was thinking that maybe, just maybe, he could go find it and show it to his sister and scare her a bit. "Is it in the waste basket?"

"No. I asked him to pick it up and take it outside somewhere and throw it away. It is probably under a foot of snow right now."

"Did he pick it up with his hand?" You could see the excitement in Josh's face.

The New Book

"No. I gave him a dust pan to use. So he scooped it up and took it out."

"Too bad. He should have used his hands and got that smell on it. His mother would have been scared by the smell."

"You know Josh, I don't think he would have told his mother. I think the man was about sixty years old."

"Wow, you mean people get that old and still come to get haircuts?"

"Lots of men do."

At that point in time an older man did come into the shop for a haircut. The guy was at least fifty or more. The boy said quietly, "Now that is old!" He started to giggle a bit under his breath.

"You know, Josh, there are a lot of men that age in town."

"Really?"

At this point the mouse story was no longer the focal point of the discussion. Somehow the discussion just automatically switched. Again Robin directed the conversation to hold the boys attention. As long as he talked a bit, he would sit still.

"You know I hate school. It is boring."

"Why is it boring?" asked Robin.

"Well you have to study and be quiet and do homework and things like that. I don't like math."

"Are you good at math?"

"No, I don't like it. My sister likes math."

He recalled that his sister was sitting in a chair at the windows and she looked at him. She seemed to say, that is right. I like math. The voice seemed to be lost in the other conversations in the barbershop. By this time two men were getting haircuts and they were having their own discussions about world events that impacted the Center of the Universe – Winfield.

"Tell me more about the mouse. How did it die?"

"Well, I put out poison and they eat it and they die. At first they think it tastes good and then they die." One of the other barbers came over to authenticate the story. Now it was real with two people telling the same thing.

"Really. Did you have to stomp on it or anything?"

"No. It was dead."

"Have you ever stomped on a mouse?"

Trying to change the conversation again, Robin asked, "Tell me, have you ever gone fishing with your dad?"

"Sure. Plenty of times. You know what I like best about water?"

"What might that be?" said Robin.

""I like pirates."

"Oh, like Blackbeard and those ships with the black flags with skulls."

"No, I was thinking about the new pirates that get on ships and shoot people with rifles and take the captain prisoner and ask for money."

The New Book

"Oh, are you talking about the captain in the new movie? I would think that would be scary."

"Yeah and cool."

Looking up Robin asked if the boy saw the movie with Tom Hanks playing Captain Phillips.

"Yeah. I saw it. The pirates killed some people and took the captain away. That was cool. They had rifles and things. There were some explosions with big red and orange flames."

Grandma said something about the family seeing the movie and Josh was not really too scared.

At this point the boy started to wiggle almost beyond control.

"What's the matter?" asked Robin.

"My ear itches."

Robin rubbed the boy's ear. Then the boy took his hand out from under the cloth and itched it himself.

"Don't do that," said grandma.

"But my ear itches." Robin rubbed it again. There was some satisfaction for a minute or two. Then the boy reached out and rubbed his nose. "My nose always itches when I get my hair cut."

So now Robin had to rub the ear and the nose. She did that several times in the next few minutes. Then she took her soft, little brush and went over his face and ears a couple of times. At this point the boy seemed to relax and did not make another move to itch any of his body parts. Grandma was relieved.

The hair cut was coming to an end. Josh sat still for a few minutes as Robin did the last touches of the hair and straightened out those last few hairs that seemed to stick up. Then one last comb through the hair and the cut was done. Grabbing a mirror, Robin turned to boy toward the big mirror and asked if he approved of the cut.

"Yes. I look just grand!" Then he itched his nose one more time.

"Well let me lower you to the ground level before you jump out of the chair."

The boy waited patiently as the chair went smoothly down towards the floor. In the silence of that last minute, Josh's sister came over and offered Josh a round ball of bubble gum. In a complex motion of the chair descending and the removal of the cloth over the front of his body, the gumball fell to the floor landing exactly where the dead mouse had been. Robin picked it up quickly to throw it away.

With a look that was somewhere between confusion and disgust, Josh wondered why Robin would waste a perfectly good gum ball. He would have chewed it.

"I am sorry, Josh, there is no five second rule here!"

Grandma gave an approving smile. Soon the three were out the door and Robin would soon engage another patron and start the conversation all over again. Would the next full grown man like to talk about the dead mouse?

Josh stood on the front porch of the barber shop for a few minutes and looked around to see where that mouse might have gone. Seeing nothing, he relented and followed grandma to the car. Perhaps when the thaw came he would find it! Who knows?

Chapter 5

The Winter of our Malcontent

In any barbershop around the country you can hear people talk about a few topics. In fact if you are a betting person you would lay odds that you could hear two of three topics as you enter a barbershop. And about eighty-five percent of the time you would win your bet. Topics discussed are the safe ones of sports, weather and the latest hot news item that occurred in the next town over. I think that weather is probably the most talked about.

No matter what the conditions are someone will have an opinion. If the weather is nice and has been for a few weeks, the pessimist will say, "Just wait!" The optimist will carry on like spring is eternal and nothing has ever happened that he could remember that was adverse. You might just ask yourself which of these two you want to hang around or in a few cases, which one are you.

On certain days I can be both. While I try to hide the curmudgeon that is hiding inside me yelling at times to get out and express itself and embarrass me one more time, I do find that I can hold back the pessimism a bit more now that I am getting older. There are any number of older men who can't. If you wander into the barbershop during the middle of a conversation that is occurring in one of the four chairs, you might not be able to tell who started the conversation. But I am guessing that one of the ladies did and in a few times wished that she had taken a safer topic.

I will suppose for this story that one's opinion of weather is somewhat related to age. When I was a young pup, I didn't really care too much about snow fall. If it came, I would deal with it. In fact in my mid-twenties, snow provided a good deal of recreation with sledding and cross-country skiing. As I found kids one morning in my house and was wondering how that happened, I would prepare for the building of forts and snowmen. A good snowball fight was a worthy winter activity that helped with several fundamentals such as forming the correct sized projectile to launch, building arm strength and attaining good marks for marksmanship.

But I had some limits for winter. I hated it when the temperature dropped below twenty degrees. There just was no good use of cold that low. At twenty degrees one could find the right single layer of clothes for cross-country skiing and a second layer for après du ski. Below twenty it seemed that the winds howled and were down right vicious. Even the folks in Lake Woebegone, the self-same Lutherans that Garrison Keillor would talk about, would begin to grumble. So here you are in the barbershop waiting your turn to talk to the ladies. You sit there wondering which one you would get today, that is if you are not picky. Some men will only allow one of the hair babes to touch the crown of their heads. I am not a picky one and feel I just might learn a thing or two if I switch around.

So the conversations are underway and you get to hear a few snippets of each conversation and will later try to put together some of the missing parts as if you are working on a verbal jiggle saw puzzle. Good luck, I say. There are always going to be some holes that you cannot pick up. So you have half-stories and have to spin your own take on what to add to make the stories nearly full and ready for some latent book that you promised yourself to write when you got old.

So I am going to try to put together the pieces of a few stories that might have been told after the past few weeks of the snowy weekends in the Center of the Universe, aka, Winfield.

Chair one:

"You know, I really like snow, it gives me a feeling of the old days when there was a lot of snow. Lately there has been little snow and it seems that even if it snows before Christmas, the weather warms or we get a rain fall and the ground is brown .."

The conversation is mostly one-sided as the fella talks his way through the winter season. At first it is difficult to tell if he is content or malcontent. He will hide his true feelings for a while. In fact it was his intent to only talk in the third person and say, "This is what I heard, or my neighbor is grumbling." Such is the way with some who want to express themselves but don't seem to like tags.

The barber just nods her head and continues the cut. At a few times the guy will let her into the conversation. A little sentence from her will cause a new snow dam to break and words will come tumbling down like an avalanche. So the haircut will continue with the words flowing. Mind you the barber has to grab this guy's head as he gets to animated with his story.

In the end, one never knows the true feelings of this type of person. Vocal anonymity is ironic.

Chair two:

"We have a gal on our block who lives with her daughter. I have seen the both of them out shoveling after a snow and I got to feeling guilty. So I said to myself that next time it snows I will take my snow blower over and clean out her drive first."

The barber says, "That is so kind of you. I think I might ask my husband to find someone to help. It makes me feel good to have him do things like that!"

Now was that tongue in cheek?

"Anyway, this year I had my snow blower out 26 times. That is a record for me. Two years ago when I bought the machine during that one big blast, I got to thinking I would never really need this machine again. But here it is. I am grateful for it and I am guessing that my neighbor is too."

The barber nods and the guy goes on. "Seems that we have a lot of snow at the end of the drive. I use the blower and then if the snow is clumpy , I have to use the shovel. Seems to me that in this day and age, the plows should have some way of not leaving a pile in my drive as they clean the streets."

"You would think so, now wouldn't you ..." The barber just barely got that partial sentence in.

"I have to shovel the snow out. I put half it back in the road and let the plow push it into my neighbor's drive. He yelled at my dog in the fall and so I guess he deserves more snow, don'tcha think?"

The barber takes a non-position on that one. The guy next door might come in after hearing her opinion. So stay silent on the neighborhood feuds if at all possible.

This is the rule 23 in the Authentic Barbershop Etiquette book.

Chair three:

"My son has made a lot of money this season going door-to-door. He and his friend have the snow blower and a shovel and they

The New Book

have made enough money to buy the new computer they wanted. It has been a good year."

"Yes, sir, the good old white makes it very green around our house. The only thing is I have to shovel my own drive since the kid is out earning money. He told me he would do our drive for half price, but I was a bit insensitive, might I say that in public, and told him a few things about life."

"You know the worse part of winter is the frozen windshields. My windshield wipers froze to the windows and I broke a pair the first big storm. So this winter is costing me a lot of money in extras and replacements."

"I can't wait for spring when there is only flooding and no frozen pipes and such. Yes puddles are easier to deal with."

Chair four:

"I was walking my dog and his paws froze. He stops and won't move. So I have to pick him up and carry him home. I do hate that part of winter."

The barber says, "Why don't you get him some booties?"

"That seems like a lot of bother for the short time you really need them. I saw an older women who had booties of her dog. Made the dog look, well ... I guess in this PC world I can only say strange."

"Anyway, I am going to Maui in a week and I will be out of this cold and snow for a while. Pity those who have to endure the whole enchilada."

So now in the area of chair 4 the conversation twists to the warmer portion of the Earth. In some most braggadocios way, the man talks about his eleven trips as if they were some badge of courage or honor. The sand is soft and warm on the toes, the food is great, but expensive. The sand, oh, I guess I said that already. I tried five new restaurants and did the best whale watch again.

The barber shows some amount of interest in the glowing talk and says that one day she too will go. But on the coldest day of the year, this is not what she wants to hear. A good warm cup of coffee and a nice nap on the sofa with a comforter would do the trick for her.

At the end of the week, the story that made the best of the best was told in chair 2: The fella sat down and was asked if he liked the weather the town was having.

"No, I am not a fan of winter."

"I know how you feel. I don't like the cold."

"Well young lady, to be accurate it is not the cold that is measured. It is the lack of heat. You see we measure heat, not cold. Temperature is heat! Cold is just the absence of heat. So you would be more correct to say it is less hot, than it is cold."

"Okay, I'll try to remember that from now on," the barber said. "It is just that in the cold, I mean less hot times, it is also so dark."

Stopped once again in the middle of a thought, the man again corrected the barber.

"What you should have said is that it is less light. You see we don't measure dark. We measure light. So there is no dark. There is only less light."

"I'll try to remember that, too."

Now she was not willing to try to say anything else. She took a guess that this was a scientist from Fermi Lab and was just one of the science kooks. "Play it safe, girl," she said to herself.

So she finished the haircut and mentioned that she was done with this session and that she hoped to see him again when his hair lengthened. She got no return comment on that one. So she dared one more thought.

"Now it is time to change the currency in your wallet to the places in my cash register."

The scientist knew that he had made his impression and he gave a broad smile and tipped the barber generously.

The door closed on another patron. The barber looked about and said, "Next!"

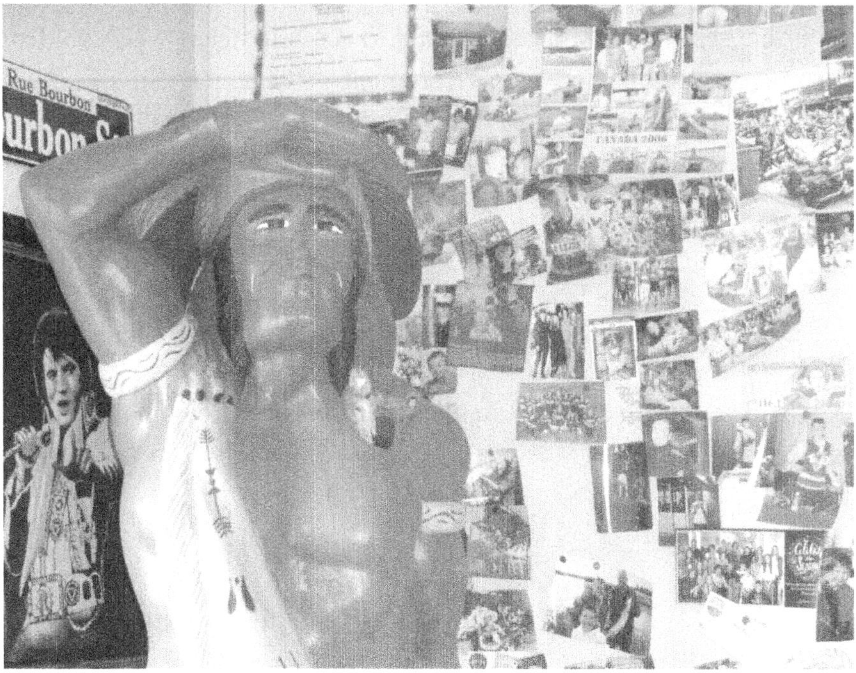
Rue Bourbon
CANADA 2006

Chapter 6

A Slow Day at the Barbershop

Fridays can bring anything at the shop. Many times the day is slow and the girls would just take turns cutting hair for anyone who came in the door. Not many came in this day wanting any one in particular to cut their hair. This was not unusual at all. It was just one of those days. Two girls sat in their chairs telling stories and passing time. One sat in one of the waiting customer chairs fidgeting with a set of keys and wondering why she didn't just go home.

The hours today were 9 AM to 5:30 PM and by 4:45 the shop only had one chair working with a teenage boy getting the last trims done on his cut. Vicki was whirling the young lad around and making small snips here and there while the boy sat quietly having nothing to say. He seemed to listen to the conversations but no one could say for sure that he was interested. A nice close haircut with a lot of trim was given since no one seemed to be in any hurry.

As with all haircuts, soon the job was done and a last look in a mirror was offered. I am not sure that anyone ever said they did not like the look of the haircut. After all is there anything you can do to get the hair back on your head that afternoon. No, you just wait a few weeks and the cut if refreshed with those delicious strands piercing from the head and making it known that another trip to the barbershop would be needed. This time a little more time would be spent tell the barber how to manage the head.

With the haircut done, the fellow left and the atmosphere became a little lighter. All kinds of things seemed to float through the air. Nothing really exciting had happened over the week, well, maybe that guy who sort of fainted in the chair and had to get a free bottle of water was worth mentioning. But nothing really came of the fainting spell and soon the guy left and the girls gave a little knowing look at each other. "Next time we need to have some strategy on how to handle things like that," said Robin.

"Well, this week we have had a lot of talk about the lost airplane. I think someone said they found it," said Robin. The guy in the waiting chair said, "No, not as of twelve minutes ago."

"Do you think it was terrorism or aliens," said Robin. "Somebody thought it was aliens. Let's face it, the airplane disappeared and no one has any idea of how or where."

This topic will ride the radio and TV for several more days, but at the barbershop, the girls seemed to care less and would only listen as customers wanted to air their thoughts. After all the barber shop is a place to provide a platform for conversation based upon what the customer wanted to air out. The girls would just provide the platform and then start the conversation, letting the customers carry most of the discussion.

It is fun to see how the people getting their hair cut can drive a conversation with the waiting customers having to play second fiddle to the activity centers. Soon the waiting people would be strapped into the platforms and could guide the conversations. Funny, isn't it?

The conversation moved on to Mardi Gras talk. How can you drink so much in such short periods of time and then just go around throwing up? One gal said, "Did you know that if you throw up in a cab in Chicago you will be fined $500.00?"

"Well if you are drunk on the street in South Chicago on Monday at the Irish Parade you will be fined $1000.00"

The discussions seemed to have no real point other than killing some time. A glance at the clock was taken and there was still thirty-five minutes to closing. Robin turned to the guy in the waiting chair, "What are you doing this weekend?"

"Nothing is happening around my house this weekend. I was out last weekend and I have to just stay around this time. I might get a special pretzel from the shop down the way as a pre-Irish party edible. Every try that place?"

"Yes, we have purchased a few of the pretzels for lunches. They were good."

"Do you like corned beef and sauerkraut?"

Jacki turned up her nose. I can guess that was her answer. Vicki said that she was going to make her own sauerkraut. She did not care for the kind out of a can. Her husband did not like cabbage but would eat the sauerkraut.

"Will you bring me some," said Robin.

"Sure, I can bring you a little bit."

Then the other Robin decided that maybe she would try for a bit of this delectable. "How about me, too?"

"There is a price for this you know. I will have to charge something. Let me see what I can come up with."

Just to show you it was a slow day, the guy in the waiting chair said, "I like your wood floor."

"Oh, isn't that great. It's Linoleum!"

"Really. It looks nice."

"You should have seen what Robin first brought in to ask if we would approve. The stuff was awful. This is pretty nice. We all seemed to think this pattern would do," said Jacki. She continued to fidget with the key and looked at the clock. Soon she could leave.

"I am not doing anything tonight. We just stay at home. Then my husband takes me out to dinner on Saturday. That seems to be our routine."

There seemed to be no response to that. Vicki thought about things for a minute and then said, "Does anyone want a glass of wine?"

"Not if it is cheap kind that you brought in last time."

"No, I wouldn't do that again. That stuff was really inexpensive, about the cost of a beer."

There were no takers. Three girls sat in the barber chairs sort of waiting for the closing hour. The conversation turned to the routine for the weekend. The owner told Jacki that she should leave the dirty towels after the day tomorrow.

Vicki said, "Don't let Gina mess up my chair."

The day might have ended at this point but a man walked in and there was a discussion about who should do the cutting. Robin II got the job. The man sat in the barber chair and before the conversation could get going a second man was coming up the stairs. It seemed like a good time for the guy sitting around killing time to go home.

Friday was a slow day.

Chapter 7

Beaufort, South Carolina

Dateline: September 26, 2014 – Beaufort, South Carolina

Today this sleepy little coastal area became the center of an Air Force Reunion that pulled together participants from as far away as Winfield, Illinois. The mayor seemed overjoyed that someone who lived in the Center of the Universe would even deem it in the realm of possibilities to travel this far. The city council had heard about the reunion from the planning committee and had brought this important meeting up to the people.

"Are you in favor of having Viet Nam Veterans come to our fair city to hold a reunion?" The overwhelming response in the last council meeting was very favorable. Banners would be put up around town and each establishment would get itself ready for the group as it came hurling into town to enjoy southern hospitality and better yet, spend money. Yes, the economy needed a big thrust and these veterans were known for spending fast and furious and not look back one little bit.

Wells Fargo was put on notice that they would need to send in two or three trucks to carry the money to Fort Knox as the shift in monetary resources was about to occur. It had been many years since an event this big had happened in Beaufort. Many on the city council could hardly remember the whirlwind events as Forrest Gump was filmed in this otherwise lazy little town. Now they would simply play catch-up with that spirit that wove their grandparents together tighter than a hot pretzel. Where would they put the mustard this time? It is just unthinkable to have a good hot pretzel without a good hot mustard for the top. A committee would be developed to figure this important detail out. The mayor commissioned the committee and gave it three weeks to bring in a report. Tomorrow was the deadline and the anticipation of the place for the mustard was causing all kinds of havoc within the business community.

So now the day was almost at hand. The sleepy little town did not seem to exist anymore. Everybody was wandering about adjusting things. In the streets kids were dancing to the music that was now being piped in to enhance the street party that would take place on the first day of the reunion.

One of the local residents had called her sister in Winfield, Illinois, and mentioned that the town of Beaufort was getting ready for this event. While the woman did not actually live in Winfield, it was easier to call her in the daytime hours than try to catch this woman later in the evening as she made her rounds of Plano, Illinois. Plano, like Beaufort was a bit sleepy most of the time. DeKalb County seemed to only get hectic during the corn Tassling Daze or the Corn Boil at the Sandwich Fair. Now talk about a hoot, you would not miss Sandwich, even if you had a broken leg. Someone would come and get you and roll you into the fair and use you as an excuse to get a front row seat at the tractor pull. It was a good thing that you didn't violate any Handicap Privileges at the fair. Farmers are most forgiving except when the tractor pulls are on.

The New Book

Well, anyway, Madeline called Robin and said, "You need to come down here, Robin. The reunion starts tomorrow. Every place on Main Street, every square inch, I do believe is taken up with a chair or a set of ropes. People set out chairs and ropes and take pictures of the areas so they can go to court if someone takes their place. It is so strange to see town folks in such a big huff."

"The Governor has sent in his representative to sit all night in a chair so he will have his own front row seat. Can you imagine that? It is true, I do-o-o declare it so."

After a few frantic moments on the telephone, Robin was able to get her sister to calm down a bit. They would have some time to talk about the Good Old Days in Beaufort. Robin would visit her sister about every summer and they would travel around to see the important sights. Beaufort had a lot of antebellum houses, but was never as significant as Savannah or Charlestown. Well, it was hard to compete against those towns directly on the ocean with nearly perfect ports for ships. In the early days, there was enough draft for the tall-sailed ships and the ports were important. As time moved on and the ship became larger, the ports were dredged to allow them to continue to operate. So each of the towns stood tall in water craft and shipping. Beaufort remained sleepy.

All that ended when Beaufort was chosen as a movie set site for movies. In a list provided by the town, over 22 movies had been filmed in and around Beaufort, including Forrest Gump, The Great Santini, The Big Chill, G.I. Jane, and Rules of Engagement to name a few. The sleepy town had charm with its tree lined streets with hanging Spanish Moss and was readily available and friendly to the Hollywood folks. The locals did not seem to know that they could have demanded more from the movie companies as they moved into town and disturbed everyone's way of life for five to six weeks and then left just as suddenly as they came.

So Beaufort went from the sleepy town that was settled around 1709 when the town located on the site of the former Cree Indian village, Cwarioc, meaning "fish town" to a local tourist hot spot for a short summer season before the hurricanes would sweep through the area. Early owners of the small town at the west end of the land surrounded by the Core Sound, known today as Taylor's Creek and the Newport River, had set down their markers determined to make this a long-term home.

One interesting item found in its history concerns the life of privateers, or pirates, you might say. In the late 1600s the ruse of tying a lantern about a horse's neck and walking along the shore with it to lure ships at sea on to the banks, where they could be scuttled and robbed. Presumably the victims believed the lanterns were the stern lights of another ship, which they would follow for safety. The name Nags Head, from the horses or "nags," is supposed to have derived from just such a practice.

Pirates had been roaming the Atlantic coast for years with bases in the Bahamas. Edward Teach, better known as Blackbeard, was one of the more infamous. Stede Bonnett, a gentleman by birth and well educated, was one of Blackbeard's lieutenants and they had friends everywhere in Virginia and in North and South Carolina. Occasionally pirates would come into the Pamlico Sound to visit and resupply. Some people were indignant that these pirates were allowed to roam so freely and were tolerated by government officials.

Recently, almost 300 years after the incident, the wreckage of what is believed to be Blackbeard's ship, the Queen Anne's Revenge, was discovered by divers in the present Beaufort inlet between Shackelford Banks and Bogue Banks. Artifacts are being brought to the surface, cleaned, preserved, and displayed at the North Carolina Maritime Museum in Beaufort.

The New Book

Can there be any more reason to hold a Reunion in this place than these fanciful tales?

Perhaps two of the best known antebellum homes in the area are Oriental Plantation and Stone Plantation. A very colorful name is provided for one of the largest plantation in the area. Pick Pocket Plantation, located in Beaufort, SC, dates back to the mid-19th Century. Owner, John Keith, takes great pride in preserving the plantation's authentic beauty. Spanning 15 acres, the property boasts 9 historical buildings, including the beautifully restored plantation home. Period antiques can be found throughout the home and property.

Historic Pick Pocket Plantation is the site of the first farm that became the Trask Family truck farming empire in the Beaufort, South Carolina area. The property was owned for almost 100 years by the Trask family, the patriarch of whom was George W. Trask, Sr., as the first acreage of what became their truck farming empire of thousands of acres of farmland surrounding Beaufort. Unfortunately the origin of the plantation name is lost to history.

The beaches in the area become hard as the tide goes out and one can ride a bicycle or ride a horse on the hard sand at the interface of the ocean and sand. The broad beach is just a fun place to play in the warm sun. More than ten thousand dreams have come true on these beaches as young men and women sealed their intents for the future and wrote love letters in the sand. Soon the waves might erase the messages, but hearts would hold true.

Well, anyway, Robin would recall with great relish the days spent in Beaufort and Charlestown as if the two were almost the same place. The town squares were still the center of tourist actions and take offs for tours. The open markets provided wholesome food grown locally. Boiled peanuts were a savory favorite as well as peach anything. In Georgia for instance, if you put peach marmalade on a shoe, someone would eat it! The folks in Beaufort would make sure the shoe was at least boiled first.

The years have gone by for Robin, but the memories remain strong. She is willing to tell you about almost anything in the area. And if pushed hard enough she just might give you her sister's phone number so you could call ahead for a recommendation of a great place to stay in a cozy B&B. Let your love lamp shine and take the trip. An old fashioned vacation will soothe your soul.

Tomorrow, the Reunion will begin. If you can stop by, please do so. And remember to say thanks to the vets for their service!

Written at Casa Blanca, February 14, 2014

Chapter 8

Holding Down the Shop

 A blustery day that came right out of the Hundred Acre Woods descended on Winfield on Wednesday. You just might expect Eeyore to come stumbling down the sidewalk looking about with no real intent or obvious needs for the moment. The early rain was taking down some of the last snow that had fallen over the last sixteen weeks and by eleven o'clock the rain had turned to 'off and on' and had no promise that the sun might come out to smile on the good people of town.

 Spring was only one day away and the streets in Winfield were mostly deserted. So daylight was going to be about twelve hours and the darkness would fill the other eighteen hours of this day. Dreary days seem longer, don't they? The fog and rain must have stopped the trains at some other place since while I was at the barbershop not a single train went through town. That is a pretty rare thing I thought as I sat getting my hair cut. Most trains stop across the Winfield Road crossing cutting the town into two pieces like this place was in its own personal Civil War Battlefield. And again I was in the Union Army. Third time in my life for that!

Entering the shop I was greeted by two gals. One, Robin II as I call her, was cutting hair of a gentleman. I could tell by the pile of hair on the floor that there was little traffic here today and the current client had little need for a haircut by my standards. The other gal I had never met before. So I asked her name and it corresponded with a wood plaque hanging on the wall. It was Gina. So now I had a name and a person together in my mind.

"So tell me, I have never seen you here before. How long have you worked here?"

"I have worked here three years. I used to work on Saturday only. Now I work Wednesday and Saturday."

I noticed a reddish tint in her hair but I have decided not to mention that fact. So please brush over this statement and go on! Well, let's see. Gina stood about five six, maybe and had an ovoid face with medium deep set eyes. There was a calmness about her that betrayed that she had spent a number of years mopping up after several children, so not many things would fluster her.

"Well, I suppose that is why I have not seen you."

"When do you normally come in?"

"I don't normally come in, I guess that is the thing. I don't really like haircuts and I wouldn't shave either, but now when I see the grey beard I mentally need to shave. I don't want to look like General Lee. After all I live north of the tracks."

I handed Gina the story I had written about Slow Fridays. "Oh, so you're the one who writes."

"Yes, I am." I guess that some of the group of five had at least looked inside of the cover of that book I left behind – Brownstone IV. And to my surprise I saw it standing up on the counter behind Gina with no indication that any pages had been dog-eared. So I might write, but I am not read! I have given thought to cutting off an ear like Vincent Van Gogh. He had only sold two paintings before he cut off his ear and had 1,100 painting sitting around in his mother's house. She was getting a bit upset about all of the drippings on the floor. My wife told me that I was dripping, too. Can someone explain that?

But that is not why I came down here today. I was looking for a story. With the barbershop mostly empty I was sure that I would not find a story. Robin just looked at me and let me talk on with Gina. She was quiet and soon after she finished her part of the day, sat in a chair and played with her ephone. The fellow she had just finished had made a few remarks about the weather and that it might be good to write about spring coming and the rain. I was not too keen on that kind of thing.

I thought, "Another slow day!"

The lighting in the shop was low and seemed to melt in well with the outside lighting. But at least the walls held back the winds that would come and go as evidenced by that piece of paper I saw swirling about across the street in the commuter parking lot. Wind is a funny thing if you sit and watch the effects of the moving air. In the poem 'Night Before Christmas' the author tells you something about air movements when he said, a few things about winds as a hurricane making leaves rise off the lower parts of the scene and rise to the sky when they met an obstacle.

I am not allowed to quote phrases from that story totally intact, so let your mind just jump in and see if the phrases come to you.

"So how come there are only two of you today?"

"Jackie took the day off. So we are holding down the fort."

"I guess that is alright since the weather is poor and there is no real traffic around town right now."

"You know my daughter wants to be a writer."

"Good. I didn't get started until I was old. Now I write every day for a few hours. It takes that some times. You just set a pace and stay with it."

She said, "I would like to be a writer. Do you write poems?"

"Yes, I have a book of poems called 'From the Heart.'"

"I don't understand poetry."

"Most poems don't have hidden meaning. They are just statements. You might have to find hidden meaning in poems in High School. It is just the punishment the teachers have for some of us not reading the likes of that boy on his sled trying to kill himself," I said.

Then to prove my point I started to quote 'Stopping By Woods on a Snowy Evening' by R. Frost.

"Whose woods these are I think I know
His house is in the village though
And he will not see me stopping here
To watch his woods fill up with snow ..."

I could have gone on, but all I wanted to say is some poems are just simple statement. But underneath that poem a lot of wild brained idiots have tried to give it meaning. Robert must still be laughing at these self-proclaimed wonders to the literary world. (Notice the ending pattern of a, a, b, a – of course you do. Your teacher told you to look for this type of thing and then gave it some name that you have long forgotten.)

The New Book

Our discussion went over the simple opportunity to write and self-publish. Time will tell if the daughter gives it a try. You have to actually write something and then try to self-publish. I waited a lot of years to get my mind in the right context.

So I thought I might make a statement about the weather here versus the everyday weather in Scotland. Today is much like what I think every day is in Scotland. It is cool and wet and a nice jacket is needed. But Scotland is a fun place to visit. You just have to have the right jacket and attitude.

It seems like when you talk about Scotland a lot of people say they went to England and it was too bad they did not have time to go to Scotland. "I heard it was beautiful up there!"

"Yes, it is! And it has distilleries. Beside they know how to spell whisky. Notice they don't use an 'e'?"

"Well maybe next time I go that way." The resignation in the voice seems to say, "I probably will never go that way again." That is too bad. I know very little about England and a little about Scotland. I could live in Scotland. England has one great feature that I think everyone should aspire to see. Haddrain's Wall was built by Roman soldiers (and English slaves?) about 100 AD to keep out the northern horde – the Scots. Much of this wall still exists as a fortification or as perimeter stone fences to keep the sheep from rebelling. (Again I am reminded of R. Frost and 'Mending Wall') *'Something there is that doesn't like a wall, and sends the frozen ground swell under it and spills the upper boulders in the sun, making gaps even two can pass abreast ...'*

So Robin continued to set in the chair and was listening to the chatter. She had little to say today. I guess that there must be some unofficial policy about one barber talking to another barber's client. So she stayed quiet keeping the code.

But the good thing is if you glance sideways at one of the other barbers in the shop as you talk to your barber is that one of them will smile if they hear a person who is sitting over a chair or two say something funny, they will at least smile. If it is really funny they might even laugh.

Well, it seemed like two barbers was about the right level of employment today. One new client came in just as I was leaving. I missed his story. I'll bet it was better than the one just above!

Chapter 9

County Fair Week at the Shop

 July can be hotter than a firecracker most years and if you stand close to a cornfield you may even hear the stalks growing and forming those little kernels that you may soon be eating. It is a time of being lazy and laid back, which is far different I'll have you know than being lazy. Most small kids probably would not know the difference, but in the mind of someone who has made a determination on any given day, there is significance in the direction they take doing nothing!

 About twice each week I have that feeling that I just want to be laid back. If I was lazy I would have stayed in bed. But I got up and made a cup of coffee and then wandered around thinking that there had to be something that I could sort of ignore and put on my list of thing accomplished. Now a lazy person would not try to find things to ignore, would he?

 So here I was on a Thursday, planning my non-activity for the day. I would at least walk the dog and I would wait until 10 o'clock and go to the vegetable stand and buy some sweet corn for dinner. If my wife had anything planned for me for the rest of the day I would go get a haircut and see how much time I could eat up at the barbershop.

The night before, I went to bed a little later than usual. As I went upstairs I could hear the boom of fireworks somewhere. I had not thought about it much and really since it was so close to the Fourth of July I thought some guy was getting rid of inventory. I had no idea that the County Fair had started and had a big fireworks display. I think that you might call me lazy on that accord since if I had looked out the window I probably would have seen the skyrockets. I am only four blocks from the fair grounds. So, now I have put myself in both categories and in one day!

Morning came and all was quiet. I still did not think about any fair going on in what was pretty much my own backyard. In my effort to stave off the 'honey do list' I decided to use the old barbershop routine. "Honey, I need a haircut before I go on our trip. She would have to agree since I had let the sexy white hair on my head get a bit over the ears and down my neck. Zoom I was off before she thought about it.

At midday I anticipated a line of cars at the shop, but was surprised by only one along the street parked horizontal and then another parked on the grass in front of the shop. That is weird. There must have been a large number of people at one time I figured. I took one of the four empty places along the road and danced up the stairs and into the shop.

As I entered I said, "Are you auctioning off that car on the lawn?"

A quick response came in a low voice. "No, it is slow and we are trying to wash our cars. It only takes four minutes. But we have had a few interruptions and have not finished the first one yet."

Four chairs and sometimes no waiting was probably a good way to describe the shop on a normal day at noon. That is why I chose this time. I expected a bit of a wait. I wanted to just listen to

The New Book

folks tell their darkest secrets so I could put them in the pages of a new book, just like the one you are now reading. So be careful what you say when you are in a chair, someone might be listening besides Big Brother or the IRS.

There was one guy getting the last part of his cut and three empty chairs. So there was not going to be any wait today. Well, I can live with that once in a while. I supposed that there would be no story unless I could get the two gals talking about the day and that car on the grass.

"Light day, today, huh?"

"The weeks before and after the County Fair are always slow. People just seem to have some other things to do and haircuts get put off. It has always been that way. Since it is slow the boss takes a vacation. She is in Mexico now."

So now in my mind the whole car wash thing was beginning to make some sense. The boss is away and instead of perhaps doing a few chores around the place, the gals were washing cars and perhaps even 'detailing the insides.'

"I used to wash my car every week," one of the gals said. I am not going to say it was the one who parked her Pontiac on the lawn. That would give away her identity and I don't want to do that for heaven's sake.

"Now I am getting lazy and I haven't washed the car for some time. Today is a good day for it. Pretty sky and all. I can get the bugs off of it. Probably. I'll get a lot more on it as I drive home this afternoon. (Hint to the ownership: the owner lives in Somonauk!)

I should have been a little quicker. The gal lives in Somonauk and drives a Pontiac. Huh! Pontiac was the chief of the

Ottawa Indians and after a while passed through Illinois as he tried to organize Indian factions against the British. I could only say that I knew there were a lot of known Indian activities in Plano and Somonauk. A weak statement that I now wish I had just ignored. Besides the statement did not lead to any follow up that I could use in the story. I might just delete this part.

I moved on to try to provoke something. I used to go to the Sandwich Fair (DeKalb County Fair, in truth) when I was younger. I moved from Batavia and had a few kids and it became harder to go with kids in school.

"Well, it is still the same week as Good Old Days here in Winfield. Right after Labor Day," came a voice from behind me.

I was plotting my story line at the time and I did not want to say anything adverse since that person had a straight razor at the back of my neck. I can see the headlines in the News of COTU (The Center of the Universe). **INSULTS LEAD TO RAGE.** I could have been a victim of my own stupidity.

Thinking that the barber pole the symbol of all shops is a red and white striped pole, I knew the history of a shop in the olden days being a place where you got haircuts, leech bleeding, and surgery. Do you want to allow some gal to try a new tooth extraction technique on you starting from the back of your head? If not learn to stay quiet and not insult the barber or her home town.

If you figure out who this gal might be, stop in and ask her about the cooler in the back of the car. You might get a good laugh out of it.

Chapter 10

Cucumber Salsa

A slow day at the barbershop and Vicky had time to have a few bites of her lunch after she finished a cut. She would take time to clean up later since there was bound to be a few more cuts today, even on a slow July day. With only two gals in the shop and one head to be brought down to size, a quick dive into the cooler to pullout a fresh cucumber salsa was in order.

I asked if it was fresh salsa without thinking through that question. Of course it was. No one cooks cucumbers that I know of. I might have to consult a cookbook, but I am pretty sure that you don't cook them.

Vicky brought the small container of salsa over to give me a look. It was mostly green with a few red spots here and there. An old family recipe to be sure that could be thrown together with ease and then let the refrigerator and the ingredients work their magic. I know that step well since I rely on it to make infusions of things that I call potato salad and summer coolers.

I am guessing that I don't have to explain potato salad to most of you. Everybody has their own way of making it with and without mustard and/or mayonnaise. I have started to use less mayo and a good dash of Italian dressing to lubricate the mixtures. A little time in the refrigerator helps to blend the different ingredients and enhance one or more of them while making others less noticeable. It is a veggie war out there and there are winners and losers to be sure.

While I spouted out my recipe, I was told that the best was made with Greek Yogurt. It is not as creamy, but has a wonderful taste overall – says the entrepreneur. Well, I have never tasted it that way, I think, so I just said, "Interesting!"

"So, tell me about the cucumber salsa!"

"I put in onions, green peppers, cucumbers, basil and a bit of tomato. I mix it up and put it in the refrigerator to allow it to mellow. And this is the result."

I must admit that it looked good and I would have liked to have a bite. I am sure that I will have to make my own since I was not offered a bite. There was little in the container at the time and the other gal in the shop noted that there was little else to eat in the shop. Someone was going to have to make a run out to the Gnarly Knot to get a pretzel. That certainly put a thought in me. After I got done, I was going across town for a pretzel. Thanks for the idea!

I got to thinking. "Hey, here is an idea! If you wash a car and then drive it to the pretzel place you will be drying it. Two things in one trip."

There was a lot of excitement in the shop. Both gals were jumping up and down with excitement. The windows began to shake, rattle and roll. I tell you the whole down town area of COTU was going to be rockin'.

The whole idea soon fell apart as the bell on the door rang once more and a new customer walked in. Vicky had to focus on the job and get herself ready to engage a new customer. Somehow in barber school the folks have learned how to be people oriented. The customer was engaged at the door and would be putty in her hands until the bill was paid.

While that sounds a bit rough, I want to say that people return week after week, except me, to be groomed by the gals of the Sportsman. They should be featured in BarbersOnlyMagazine. Come in and sign a petition that we can send to the magazine asking that they be recognized for 'Being a Cut Above' in their quirky kindness.

And look on the internet for a good Cucumber Salsa recipe.

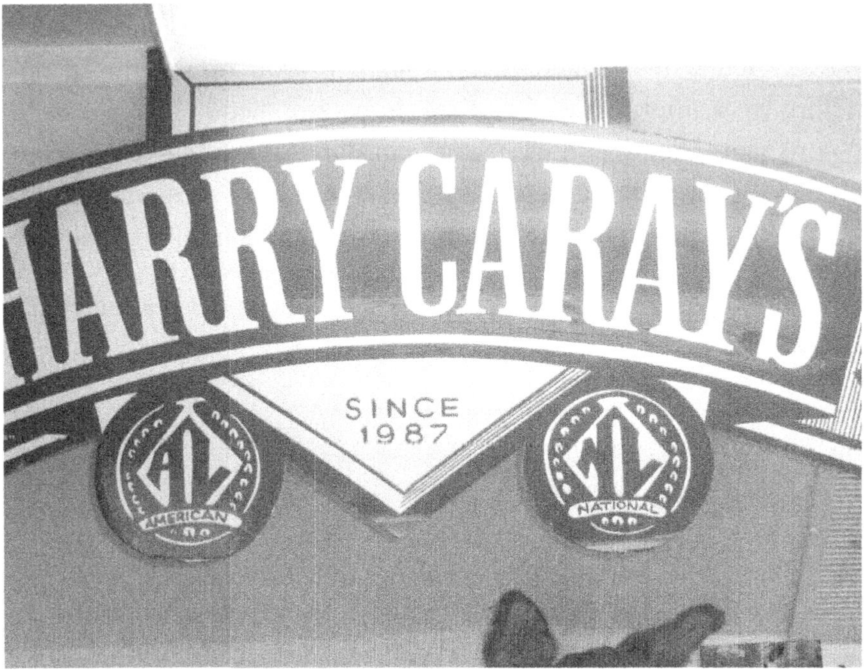
HARRY CARAY'S
SINCE
1987
AMERICAN
NATIONAL

Chapter 11

Equality

There are few places in this world where one can go and find that they are equal to anyone else in the place they enter. In the first days that coffee reached into England that place was a coffee house. Even though you might think that no one in their right mind in England would drink coffee when they had all of those marvelous teas, you need to know that coffee became the unique drink of the mixed population around the country.

Coffee was brought into England and unlike chocolate, it was used by all strata. The coffee house is a place where you could go and rub shoulders with the rich or poor, tell stories of any kind and be treated like a right jolly bloke with no other thought behind the thought.

Well, to me it seems that there are two places in America that are similar in feeling and spirit. One is the hair stylist for women and the other is the barber shop which can be used by either sex. As I have told a few people about the current project of writing 'Tales of the Barber Shop', I have been told by the fairer sex that the same things occur in the beauty salons. Now I am not a bit surprised with that statement.

The two places are generally the same in size and structure in that there are a row of chairs where a person can be served for whatever is in order. A person is serving and another is being served. So far things are just the same. Let me call it equality for right now.

As in the olden days coffee houses, and certainly not today's Starbucks, I will get into that issue in a minute, the two places are like a petrie dish where the germs of discussion are growing and tales and gossip abound. While it might be that only two persons are involved in any discussion if you stop to think about it, you would be wrong. The truth is that what is said in the shops is a kind of universal truth and knowledge that is not going to be hidden any longer. People will tell their life histories and gab about their likes and dislikes. A lot of talk buzzes about the current events, weather, sports and politics. For the most part religion is often considered taboo.

So let's just go back to the Starbuck comment for a second and then go on if time allows. In Starbucks there are tables set up for people to use. The stores all seem to have Wifi and this is the conversation killer. You can sit right next to a person for an hour and never talk to them as your finger fly around the little pads hitting various symbols that we have borrowed from the old time Muslims. We call it alphabet these days. And the ultimate thing that seems to happen is when two teenagers, makes no difference if they are boys or girls, sit across a table from each other and text back and forth. They never even look up at each other as they spill out the day's worth. Sort of puts you into a funk to know that we no longer need to talk. Soon we will be able to just telecommunicate like the aliens we always see in the movies. They never seem to talk but totally have learned to use their minds for what they need to do. And in the movies humans begin to think of the aliens as a 'higher life'. I am

The New Book

not so sure that we would consider what goes into a text as communications by a higher life.

Well, anyway, Starbucks does not pass the old English test of equality. It is on some standards a place of equality with people of all strata moving in and out, but since there is no interaction, the equality factor cannot be measured.

While I am not an expert in the communications area and my wife accuses me often of not communicating, I can tell you that I observe several patterns of interaction occurring in the barber shop. I have not sat in a beauty shop so I am not going to extend my comment. That is for others to do as they see fit.

I see the communications between two persons and then the four person quick step as two chairs of clients and the cutters work the stories back and forth. You must know that it takes a special barber to get this type of communication going and then to sustain it for fifteen minutes. I have witnessed this great skill in one of the barbers in the Sportsman Barber Shop. Indeed this person with skill is often sought after for ability to get a conversation going that takes the boredom out of the haircut. So when a person comes in for a haircut, he might just wait for the right opening. Each person seems to be able to bring about a conversation with the 'right barber.'

So you ask, now who is that person? Well, just observe and figure it out for yourself. You might come up with the same person. Maybe not.

But in an equal system, twos, fours, fives and maybe more can get into a conversation about some hot topic. One of the chairs might provoke the discussion and let the chips, no the hair clippings, fall where they may. Children are just as important as grown men. There is a non-numbered system that comes into play as a person enters a barbershop. You look around and see who is sitting waiting for a haircut and just hunker down thinking about when it will be your turn. Sometime you don't get it right. A person, certainly not me, will look like he has no reason to be in the shop unless he sits waiting for one of the guys in a chair to be finished so they can go play horseshoes or something. Then when a chair is empty, this person who needs no haircut gets up and goes to the empty chair, I just say 'Go figure!'

But the point is a ten year old boy has the same rank and privileges as the seventy year old man. They both wait patiently for their turn. One could be a corporate CEO, while the older one is semi-retired! And the barbers will treat the ten year old boy like a man. "Can I trim your beard?" one of the ladies will say to the young boy.

There is a little titter that goes around the shop as the boy considers this new status. He says, "Can I view it first in the mirror before I spend my hard earned money?"

The mirror is waved in front of him and he shrugs a bit and says, "No, it makes me look distinguished, don't you think?"

Now there is equality!

Chapter 12

Skunked

It happens in the suburbs often enough. One day you realize that you are sharing space with a skunk. To many people that is not a pleasant thought. You think about what an encounter might bring to you and perhaps your dog. The thoughts are less than pleasant I can assure you. I have had some of those over the years and as I look back on the thoughts I have mixed emotions.

Robin had a skunk skin brought into the barbershop just a short time ago. It now hangs on the south wall from a horn of some other beast and does not really have much appeal. But in a sense where there are so many other animal heads and bodies (fish) around, the skin, in and of itself, is not really out of place. The black and white stripes just sort of add to the overall eclectic feel of the Sportsman Barbershop. So I saw it and only had a short comment.

"I see you got a new creature there!"

"Yes, I got it a few weeks ago."

That part of the conversation did not get any follow up I am sad to say. So I cannot report who brought it in or how it came to be a skin. Oh well, I might ask the next time. But the skin did provoke a conversation.

"You know we had a skunk in our backyard once," reported Robin. "I was making its rounds all of the time and I got to feeling that one day it was going to be a problem. Since I have kids, I needed to find a way to eliminate the skunk."

I could tell that this story was not going to be a good one for the skunk. Man v. Skunk normally turns out poorly for someone. Well this time it was the skunk's turn.

"My neighbor came over and shot the skunk. You know when you kill a skunk they just seem to let go of all that stuff they have!"

Well what would you expect? I am sure if I hung a man he might do some similar thing.

"The spray went everywhere in a big arch like a rainbow. You could see it float up into the air and drift across the lawn. Soon it settled down and the smell, oh that smell, it took some time to be reduced to a low aromatic level that was tolerable."

Makes one think about what you just let happen doesn't it? It might have been better to sort of chase the skunk off property and see if you could find a way to dissuade it from returning. Well, the deed was done and there was no way of going back. So now the task is to pick up the dead creature and remove it. It has to be taken away or the smell in the garage or garbage can will continue to overwhelm you for a long time. I was given no information about disposal, but I am sure that the shooter had to take care of this task. Robin gave a hard look out the window before she went on.

"I thought that was going to be the end of it. I was wrong. That rainbow of spray that landed on the lawn soaked on to the grass and into the soil and every time it rained for a few months that smell was back. The front yard became unusable. We had to shut the front door and keep everyone in the back yard for months."

The New Book

I said, "I can imagine that. You know the scientific name for the skunk is 'Mephitis mephitis'. That is Latin for foul stench of the Earth. And it is said twice so you know that the Romans thought this creature was a bad actor."

I got no response to that. So I sat and let Robin continue to cut my hair.

"You know. I have lived here in town for a number of years and I have a fenced backyard. The shed in the yard has a propensity to collect animals that are trying to endure us humans. I have had a few skunks, three opossums, a number of rabbits and a few chipmunks in the years. I tend to just let them alone. They don't seem to hurt anyone. The skunk digs a few grubs, but the other animals just seem to abide. They are coping with us here in suburbia."

Robin finished my hair cut and somehow we got to talking about books.

"I need a good book at my bedside or I cannot sleep," she opined. "A couple of months ago I could not sleep and finally figure out that I did not have a book at bedside. When I made the correction, sleep became natural once again. Isn't that funny?"

That is good I guess. I don't try to read in bed so I never really had to address that issue. But everyone has their own way of dealing with the evening time.

"I took a book by Patterson to Maui a few months ago. I like to read a hugger mugger type thing on the trips. It is so different from what I might read otherwise and I find a good bit of mental freedom in the reading."

"I like Patterson and I like Gartner, too! Do you know her?" asked Robin.

55

"Sure I have seen her books on the shelves. She seems to have a few books out there. I have not read any so I cannot comment. For my home reading I am slowly plowing through the biography of John Adams. He and his wife were very fascinating people and I think America was established as much from his life teachings as that of Thomas Jefferson."

I did not get a lot of response to that. But then one has to think about what you find interesting and who you are. I am sure that Robin has much different tastes than this old guy has. So I push on to other things.

I can tell you that life in Winfield is like living in Lake Woebegone. The simple life style can go on in town. You can get all the excitement you need at a town meeting. The meetings are more fun than watching world wrestling. The papers in town show all the flurry of action as if the town was a three ring circus. You are left to thinking that this is not real. What is there to gain in a small town? We are a kind of Peyton Place at times. The steamy things go on and are finally allowed to be launched out into the public.

If you don't really care, you can stay at home because no matter what happens at the city meetings, there is little that actually occurs that effects daily life. The drums go silent between the meetings. When good Old Days comes, everyone is friends once again for the week.

Now if Robin would only put a table with a checker board in the barbershop, we might have somewhere to go to and spill out our woes as we watch our misplaced checkers get eaten up by the ruthless Red Baron.

Night will fall and soon the town lights will come on. That skunk's friend will try to find a new place to go at night. He knows Robin's neighbor is a problem.

Chapter 13

Rascal at the Barbershop

This morning as I was returning from the car shop where I dropped off the car for an oil change, I stopped in the barbershop with Rascal at my side. The day was beautiful and Rascal had been enjoying the new fragrances of that end of town where he hardly ever gets to walk. So he stopped at least nine times to let every other dog in the neighborhood know that he had passed that way. It is for dogs a time honored ritual and there is hardly anything a human can do to stop it, and I really think we humans don't want to.

Across the main street we went and cut through a parking lot to get one street to the south of the most direct way home. Rascal was a lot happier when we got off the asphalt parking lot and onto some grass. He stopped to roll in the fresh cut grass but had forgotten to tell me he was stopping. I felt the tug on the line and turned to see him do a double twisted backflip into the green grass just below. I would have given him an 8.75 for the effort. He would have got more perhaps if he told me he was going to do it so I could see the takeoff.

In the grass a second time he rolled left and then right. I remembered that last night we were in the television room (what have I come to that I use the idiot box for the name of the location) watching a war movie with aerial combat. I did not realize that Rascal was so absorbed in the movie until now. He moved left and right in the grass to avoid an enemy coming in and then he turned and stood to face the invisible 'it'. The invisible 'it' ran and so did Rascal. He was moving on and pulling me along behind him.

We were just a block from the barbershop. I was walking that way on purpose so I could show the girls my dog. Rascal is a nice looking, but a bit oversized, not fat, Yorkshire Terrier. He is very friendly and likes women better than men. But he will tolerate a man who will stop to pet him and tell him how wonderful he is.

The two doors on the shop were propped open so we went up the stairs and headed to the second door. All you see at the first door is the cash register and the lollipops. I want to go in that one for the lollipop, but Rascal wanted to see the 'babes' as he called them. He saw three babes this morning and a tune came to his head. If only the babes could have heard it!

'You don't have to be a Mongolian masterpiece to get alone with the beautiful babes …'

Almost in one voice the three looked and said "What a cute puppy. How old is it?"

I responded that "Rascal is four and big for his age."

One gal stooped to pet him and remarked about how nice and long his hair was. The hair on the back of Rascal's neck went up. He was turning to leave when he heard the magic in the air.

"Can I give him a treat?"

I heard, "Can I give him a tree?"

"No, we have stopped at nine trees already and I would find it difficult to carry a tree home with me."

"I said treat!"

"Oh, sure he likes treats."

Rascal already knew what was said but has become suspicious of treats since when given one out of a context of coming in from a walk it might mean going to the groomer, being left in a cage or some other fate that would make his day less than he wanted it to be.

He was handed at treat and rejected it.

"Take the treat with you for later."

"Ok, I will." And I put the treat in a shirt pocket and decided to pick Rascal up so everyone could get a good look before we headed down the street.

The other two girls would have liked to come over to pet him, but there were two seniors getting their weekly trim. They had given a look and hoped that the barber would not go to the dog and bring back lice, ebola and other things.

So with a last look around the shop, Rascal wiggled telling me it was time to go. After all Rascal is not a lap dog and really does not like to be held. Constraints are not his style.

He looked back over his shoulder, as he is wont to do, and smiled at the babes. In his mind he said, "I'll be back!"

Doug Ehorn

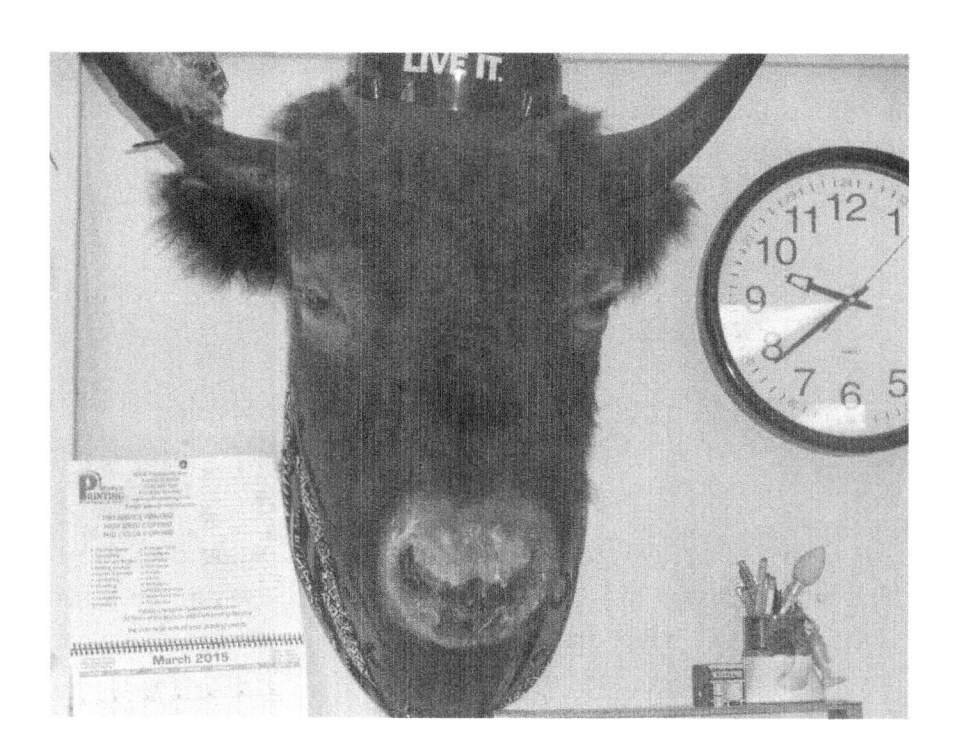

Chapter 14

Cantigny

September 28, 2013, was a day of celebration and fun at Cantigny Park in Winfield, Illinois. For those of you who have no idea of what this park with a French name is let me give you just a snippet before I get to the story.

In World War 1, also known as the Great War, Robert McCormack who was the owner of the Chicago Tribune determined that he was going to go to war. His motives were probably quite well known. He had never served in the military, but was appointed to be a Colonel in the army. While I have no idea what he did most of his time that can be learned if you wish to go seek his history. The important thing to him was that he served as some mid—level officer at a place called Cantigny, France. Having loved this place so much, when he returned to the states and proclaimed himself a hero, he decided to buy land out west of Chicago and create an estate.

The estate had formal gardens and polo fields and room for fox hunts. So you can imagine the size of the plat of land. As the years went on and the Colonel died, a foundation took over the site and has for years kept the estate open to the public for many things. It now includes the mansion which can be toured, the formal gardens that are all walkable, the special rose garden, the grave sites for the Colonel and his wife, a First Army Museum, a grove of trees with twelve tanks from various eras going back to WW1. There is now a golf course that is one of the best in Chicagoland on the areas where some used to fox hunt.

The foundation has been giving concerts and training for years. They have free concerts most Sundays in summer. They have recently developed an Honors Group for veterans that allows free access to the site and reduced prices for golf and the restaurant on the grounds. Talk about putting your money where your heart is, Robert McCormack and his foundation are right at the top of the list.

But today I went to the park and enjoyed the 5th Annual Veterans Fest. There was free entrance for all veterans even if they were not in the Honors Program. I am in the program. The food was free all day from breakfast through supper. A few free beers were allowed. But pop and water were free all day.

The fest included booths for a lot of veterans' help groups so one could talk to people about benefits and insurance and such. I don't want to go too far with trying to detail all of the organizations involved. But it was expansive.

The concert stage was going all day. I left the park about 7:30 PM and the next group was going to be playing soon. This was no rinky-dinky affair. It was a class act.

Being a Viet Nam vet I know that we had no home coming like the vets of WW1 and 2. I don't much think about that nor do I hold anyone to blame for the lack of saying to those who serve, the war was not a good thing, but thanks for putting your life on the line. As one veteran said, if we had not fought in France we might be speaking German or Japanese. Thank a veteran for your freedom. He deserves it.

Last year I was in Washington D.C. and went to a ceremony at the WW2 Memorial. There is a group that brings the WW2 vets to Washington from all over the USA. The veterans are provided transportation, lodging, food and a helper if they need one. Each day at the memorial there is a ceremony with a wreath placed by the

"Wall" with hundreds of star, each representing one hundred men. It is humbling to stand by these wonderful men and just say "Thank You!"

I could not say that enough as I walked their crowd and shook hands.

Veterans have earned the right to have some privileges and you, and that includes me, should take time to make sure that the guy down the block from you knows that you care about him and are thankful for his or her service. It should be unthinkable that a veteran might live on your block and not be known.

I can only ask that you take it to heart and just give "DAMN" about the veterans of your town. Winfield, it is time for you to get your list of the VETS together. Keeneyville, you have no excuse, all of your veterans are listed on line at this point. If you want the list posted again, just respond to this, no, better yet I will post it along with this note.

Time is fleeting for many of those who served in WW2 and Korea. Take some time now to show your gratitude.

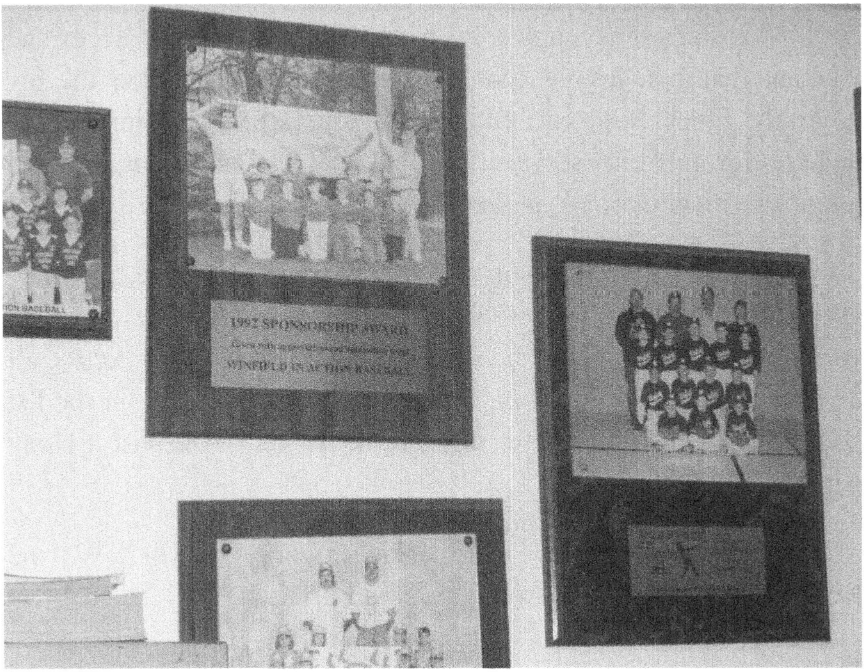
1992 SPONSORSHIP AWARD
WINFIELD IN ACTION BASEBALL

Chapter 15

Retirement: A perspective

"So how should I cut your hair? The usual?"

"Yes, that would be fine."

With that quick exchange the haircut was underway. I have no idea how a topic might come up in any one of the chairs on any day, but I find the mix of topics discussed and finally determined in the twenty minutes in the chair. It is just an extraordinary set of circumstances that makes my mind wander down the halls of the world's great theaters mesmerized by the diversity of things that can be learned or maybe just recalled as two people converse in the comfort of the barber chair. What does one expect concerning confidentiality as they dump that bucket of thought that was about to overflow.

Do people come to the barbershop knowing their bucket needs to be emptied or do they come and without any preconceived thought that they would enter into the nether world where they would not discuss the same topic with their wife or children? I wonder!

In chair one, I heard snippets of the discussion. Today it was retirement. I am going to assume that it started when the barber was just being polite and/or trying to figure out how much to charge at the end of the cut. Let me see … three dollars is on the line here!

And perhaps the thought of "If I screw up the haircut how much trouble might I be in?"

Naw, I am sure it is not the latter since we are in the realm of the professional. In the olden days you could get a haircut and have your evil blood withdrawn by leeches at the same time. That is why the barber pole has the red and white stripes, you know!

I did notice today that there was emergency equipment under the counter by the cash register! I was going to get up and leave thinking there is something going on here that I am becoming uncomfortable with. On the other hand it might be a great thing to write about if a haircut led to an emergency. Hey, the hospital is only two blocks away. It would take only six hours to get an ambulance there, quickness is important as I had witnessed at a play at a local theater just this past week. Well, I don't want to go into that. Curiously, the fire truck got to the scene before the ambulance. Everyone in the theater thought the man with the heart problem might have started some internal fire that could spread. Let's not dwell on that, we are after all talking about retirement.

"So are you retired now?"

"No, there is one little four lettered word that prevents that from happening."

I was trying to figure out what that word might be. A couple of old military words ran through my mind and I was then thinking back to the high school years. Which time did I use the worst of the words floating around? I do admit to thinking the words every once in a while, but I am pretty sure that only the most acceptable of the words are uttered these days.

"Wife!"

The New Book

The man said 'wife.' I was taken by surprise by that four lettered word. So if he retired he would have to be at home with his wife?

No, that is not where the conversation was going. If he retired right now his health insurance would go out of sight when he would pay his own premium. Premium is now the proper word for those payments. The premium bucks you have you go to pay for the great island adventures of those who shovel the dollars into their swimming poos like Scrooge McDuck so they can go swimming in the money.

"The premium that I pay now is four hundred dollar. If I have to do it alone it is double that. Maybe I could get my wife off my insurance and get a lower rate!"

Snip, snip went the scissors as the barber worked the top of the hair with her fingers and the scissors in a coordinated effort. The movements were more than functional; they were a work of art. Picasso would blanche at the art work that was coming into focus. The man would go from a man needing a trim into the model on the front of GQ Magazine. All that for just eighteen dollars.

Abiding the ever moving head of the man talking, the barber continued her rounds as if she were the postman ... neither shift nor turn nor laughing loud will deter the trimming of his brows.

"There ought to be a way that I can get cheap insurance so I could stop working. But you know I sort of like having a few things to do, so I continue and use the money to pay the piper. Life is like that I suppose."

"Yes, it is. I know that I am glad my husband has a good job and insurance. I know it can be expensive. The thing that is always on my mind is that I hardly ever use any medical service, so it is like throwing money away."

The spray of the foam lather can is heard signaling to everyone, even those in the chair waiting like me, that soon that hair cut was going to be over and people would shift around. While you could not hear it, the steel blade of the straight razor was soon at work moving up the landscape of the man's neck. One slip and the man would need that insurance.

"Now don't tell my wife I called her a four lettered word. That could cause an uproar at the house that I am not ready for. Perhaps next week I might be ready. Seems that every once in a while I need a bit of tension in the house."

"I know what you mean," the barber said. She was thinking about the last time she cut her husband's hair. He was so picky about things that she just decided to let him go to the shop in the town where they lived.

The man paid his bill and departed. The barber shook off that conversation and her covering cloth and was ready for the next verbal adventure. Where would it take her this time?

Chapter 16

How the World Works: A Perspective

I got in late on this conversation so I have no idea if other things had been discussed before I caught a few words. I came to the barbershop to actually get a haircut this time. But I must admit that I was ready to gather in a few story points to put in this book you are now reading.

The identities of people in this story are carefully protected under the Haircutting Regulations of the State. So don't ask any questions.

"There are no (political) parties in Washington. Everyone there is only interested in finding people with money so they can get reelected. Staying in office with its inherent power is the bottom line. At home highly prized phrases are thrown around that get the masses to go to the polls to reelect a person who hasn't done much for the past two years. But the reality is that in Washington, the lobbyists and their clients are running the show propping up the elected pols that we continue to send without any delay."

Aside from the author: Perhaps we are just trying to get these leeches out of town so we don't have to be around them too often.

"You know I live in a condo complex and the board there is just like the people in Washington. Conversations go on and on and nothing gets decided since no majority can be reached. I guess there are too many people on the condo board. In the absence of any new determinations the old ones continue so the grass is cut and all of that.

"It just seems that everyone at all ages just wants to have their say and many want their idea to be the one that is used. They are willing to fight for it."

The barber looked down at the man and took a deep breath. She had been cutting hair here for twelve years and has heard every nasty story that started in the village meetings here in town. For years it seemed like a civil war on Thursday evenings. It made good television and a lot of people wondered why the board meetings did not make national television. If one, only one of the board member would take off his clothes it was a shoo-in and the commercial money would flow in like a river.

"Seems like things are settling down here in town, doesn't it?"

"Perhaps for a few more months. But don't hold your breath. The war will begin again over something. There are a few persons who are holding their tongues but they have the ability to get nasty pretty quickly."

The man continued. " I can remember when we would send a man to Washington for a particular reason and we would see results. Yes, those were the real good old days. Now we have this fake thing next weekend and celebrate all the new stuff with carnivals, bean bag tosses that replaced horseshoes … Have they banned horseshoes as being weapons of mass destruction? Ah, well you know what I am getting at. What is so old about all of the things at the party in the streets? Where are the animal shows? Seems like we lost our farms and our heritage."

Not wanting to say too much but having an obligation under section 104(b)(4) of the Barber Code, the gal was obligated to at least shake her head. She had to show agreement or be fined if word ever got out. So she shook her head and then said, "I agree with you on that."

Did you ever wonder if the barber ever really listened to those things that were controversial? I do. I would not listen too well. I would sit and practice in front of a mirror to say… "I think you are right .. good point ... let me think on that one."

The man went on.

"How do we get these people to be accountable to us and not the big money?"

I don't want to take anything away from the women or men barbers, but do you think they are going to try to solve the world problems. I think not since they want to keep the shop open and try to keep politics out of the conversation. They learn to turn the conversation to something easy and noncontroversial.

"Did you get caught in that rain storm yesterday? I knew it was going to rain. My son washed his car. Works every time."

The buzz of the clipper began to drown out the man's voice and I decided to look over the crossword puzzle for the day. When it was my time to take the chair, the gal asked, "Did you bring us a story today?"

"Yes I did. And soon I will want to try to get all of you gals together outside of the shop so I can take a picture for the cover of the book. Not that I am in a hurry, but sometime before the snow falls would be good."

"Speaking of good, are you going to Good Old Days?"

"Yeah, probably tomorrow night. How about you?"

She responded, "I think I will go to the Sandwich Fair instead!"

Since I reside in Winfield I am obligated to report this to the city council. So my dear, consider your life in jeopardy!

I left her a tip since she was honest!

Chapter 17

How the World Works: A Perspective

I got in late on this conversation so I have no idea if other things had been discussed before I caught a few words. I came to the barbershop to actually get a haircut this time. But I must admit that I was ready to gather in a few story points to put in this book you are now reading.

The identities of people in this story are carefully protected under the Haircutting Regulations of the State. So don't ask any questions.

"There are no (political) parties in Washington. Everyone there is only interested in finding people with money so they can get reelected. Staying in office with its inherent power is the bottom line. At home highly prized phrases are thrown around that get the masses to go to the polls to reelect a person who hasn't done much for the past two years. But the reality is that in Washington, the lobbyists and their clients are running the show propping up the elected pols that we continue to send without any delay."

Aside from the author: Perhaps we are just trying to get these leeches out of town so we don't have to be around them too often.

"You know I live in a condo complex and the board there is just like the people in Washington. Conversations go on and on and nothing gets decided since no majority can be reached. I guess there are too many people on the condo board. In the absence of any new determinations the old ones continue so the grass is cut and all of that.

"It just seems that everyone at all ages just wants to have their say and many want their idea to be the one that is used. They are willing to fight for it."

The barber looked down at the man and took a deep breath. She had been cutting hair here for twelve years and has heard every nasty story that started in the village meetings here in town. For years it seemed like a civil war on Thursday evenings. It made good television and a lot of people wondered why the board meetings did not make national television. If one, only one of the board member would take off his clothes it was a shoo-in and the commercial money would flow in like a river.

"Seems like things are settling down here in town, doesn't it?"

"Perhaps for a few more months. But don't hold your breath. The war will begin again over something. There are a few persons who are holding their tongues but they have the ability to get nasty pretty quickly."

The man continued. " I can remember when we would send a man to Washington for a particular reason and we would see results. Yes, those were the real good old days. Now we have this fake thing next weekend and celebrate all the new stuff with carnivals, bean bag tosses that replaced horseshoes … Have they banned horseshoes as being weapons of mass destruction? Ah, well you know what I am getting at. What is so old about all of the things at the party in the

The New Book

streets? Where are the animal shows? Seems like we lost our farms and our heritage."

Not wanting to say too much but having an obligation under section 104(b)(4) of the Barber Code, the gal was obligated to at least shake her head. She had to show agreement or be fined if word ever got out. So she shook her head and then said, "I agree with you on that."

Did you ever wonder if the barber ever really listened to those things that were controversial? I do. I would not listen too well. I would sit and practice in front of a mirror to say... "I think you are right .. good point ... let me think on that one."

The man went on.

"How do we get these people to be accountable to us and not the big money?"

I don't want to take anything away from the women or men barbers, but do you think they are going to try to solve the world problems. I think not since they want to keep the shop open and try to keep politics out of the conversation. They learn to turn the conversation to something easy and noncontroversial.

"Did you get caught in that rain storm yesterday? I knew it was going to rain. My son washed his car. Works every time."

The buzz of the clipper began to drown out the man's voice and I decided to look over the crossword puzzle for the day. When it was my time to take the chair, the gal asked, "Did you bring us a story today?"

"Yes I did. And soon I will want to try to get all of you gals together outside of the shop so I can take a picture for the cover of the book. Not that I am in a hurry, but sometime before the snow falls would be good."

"Speaking of good, are you going to Good Old Days?"

"Yeah, probably tomorrow night. How about you?"

She responded, "I think I will go to the Sandwich Fair instead!"

Since I reside in Winfield I am obligated to report this to the city council. So my dear, consider your life in jeopardy!

I left her a tip since she was honest!

Chapter 18

In Between Times

My haircut is finished and out the door I go
It will be at least six weeks before again I go
To that building cozy and warm

With several chairs just a waiting
What will I do between those times
When I consider hair too long

Going about my different tasks
Assigned by the fortunes of life
The days slip away as fast as a bunny
Dodging under a fence and away from my dog

In what seems like just a moment
The morn has turned to dusk
It makes no real difference
What I had planned to do each day
But half the list completed
The sun has gone away
Leaving me to thinking
Or hoping that the sun would again rise
For I would fulfill the promises made

A trip to Carolina, a journey to the mall

All seem to fill up moments
That otherwise would be assigned
To someone else who had already used his time
And now required more

So I had better move on and use my allotment
Sharing my life with those I adore
On Thursday next
I return to the barber and put my thoughts away
And listen for some tale to inspire me
A chapter of a book displayed
For the price of a mere haircut

I came to reap a million thoughts
And let one dance until it becomes
With the wind of the morning
A droll story of life

The grey hair falls down before me
Time has passed so fast
The girls in the barbershop
Shake off the hair I grew
And tell me I am through
So now I have another chance
To pass the time between
This cut of hair and then the next
What will occur, I am vexed!

Chapter 19

Winfield Veterans of Viet Nam

The other day I was getting ready for my quarterly haircut at my favorite shop. I would guess that I am not the favorite customer at the Sportsmen's' Barber shop since I show up so infrequently. But that is my style and I doubt that I am going to change very much now that I am seventy years old. All that aside I have the two purposes for showing up there. I would like to hear a new story that someone has to tell. We are all walking stories you know and sometimes we allow others to take a peek at us in places where we don't feel too vulnerable, not physical places, but mental places. Not only are we walking stories, but we are walking secrets. I am sure that my wife of over forty years still does not know a number of things about me. She did find out a few things the other day when I wrote a story and out popped a bit of information that was not secret, but I had never talked about that particular matter.

We are all like that. If something shines a light on an area of the brain that resonates, a little factoid will pop out and take a ride around the room. Some will laugh at the experience shared, some will be devastated and others will shrug and go on with their lonely little lives not fully understanding that life is relationship, not salary and places to go. Don't get me wrong. I like to go places and now I have the islands in mind. It is February you know.

Anyway the second reason I come down to the barbershop is that I have too much money and I need to get rid of it as soon as possible. No, wait that is what my wife says, not me. Well, she left me a $20 the other day and I wanted to get a haircut so I would look like I was running for some office. I was glad the day was sunny and the temperatures were nearing 30 degrees. It make one feel good to walkout into the sunshine and let the brightness of the sun begin to warm you as you stroll down the street checking out things that the neighbors were doing. I have a good excuse. I walk the dog a couple times a day and sneak looks at activities in other yards. There can be a lot going on in winter.

Things were a bit dull here on a Friday morning and I thought that it would be good to cut the hair. Driving to the shop I pulled up behind a SUV that had a license plate that let you know the driver was a Viet Nam Vet. We need not go into what the plate said, it said enough. I walked into the shop and asked which one of the two getting a haircut was the vet. The second chair contained a man who responded. I can tell you this it was up for grabs in my mind. So I walked over to him and thanked him for his service. I had noted that he had a Purple Heart on the license plate – he had been wounded at least once.

Stretching out my hand it was met with a firm hand that was fully appreciative that his service was recognized and honored. I knew he was an Army man service with the 101st. They did more than there duty in Viet Nam and you can see their movements if you searched history. His face was jolly and he was most at ease with his past and present. I thought, "This is a fortunate man." He came home after one and one half tours, while he didn't say it he may have come home wounded during the second tour. So we talked a bit about his time over there. I had a bit of overlap in time with his service in the late 1960's. I left in 1970 and he left a year later. Now we both

The New Book

recognized that it was the 40th anniversary of the end of the war. That gives you pause when you stop to think about it.

In just a few sentences you could tell that his memories were rich and clear. The focus was all about the men he served with and not the things completed. I know that I fell the same way. When I get together with old friends we talk about our time off during the conflict and very rarely talk about what we did. Most people would not understand. They might give an 'aha' if you said you have medals, but they would not buy you a cup of coffee.

I think that most returning men did not get any good reception when they came home. There were no parades and no towns hanging banners saying that they were proud of the men who were called. Quietly the men filtered back into town and tried to fit in again. Most I think seemed to make the transition back. Some would never be the same. I knew several of those who were walking wounded.

Well, good soldiers always will have at least one story that they might pull up to show that while war is hell, there is always something that will make you laugh after the event is over. The following is based upon the short part of a story told by this man as he stood in front of my chair while my haircut was being finished:

"I was leading a patrol north of DaNang in the Achow Valley. I had a very good squad of men and we had been together a long time. We knew and understood each other and could use body language to communicate. Two things that we experienced north of DaNang was the part of a valley that seemed to be filled with monkeys. Tall, black monkeys were everywhere. They were so noisy that the cong probably did not want anything to do with this part of the valley. As we moved through the valley the monkeys would jump out of nowhere and of course it was a bit unsettling at first, jumping monkeys in a war zone. The men would have an automatic response and raised their rifles and shot the monkeys. However, the noise never seemed to drive these creatures off. At the end of the first day my team was running low on ammunition and I had to call in for a drop. The second day was pretty much the same, so again I called in for a drop. The CO (Commanding Officer) called back when he heard we had used so much ammo. What is going on?

"Well, we seem to have a monkey problem and the men are shooting first and thinking second.

"Well, tell them to remove the clips from the rifles and take one round and carry in their hand so that they start to think this over.

"Yes sir, I will tell them.

"I told them alright knowing full well that that would never happen. We all disobeyed that order, but I can tell you this, we stopped shooting monkeys. Everyone began to think.

"National Geographic has recently had a television program that talks about the monkeys in the region being endangered. I guess I have some reason to know why."

Well that was enough of a story for me, but the man wanted to give me one more thought before he left.

"One of my men got up early one morning and made it into the forest to take care of business. He took his shovel with him, but not his rifle. Having started the process that was necessary, he squatted and soon was disturbed by a noise right behind him. Army men are trained to react and he knew he did not have his rifle so he did the best he could. Picking up the shovel he swung it with all his might. The shovel hit its target and the roar of a tiger came. It did not take a look to know what had happened. The man grabbed his pants and ran pulling them up as he ran back into camp yelling. On his way he tripped over another shoveled spot. The men had heard the roar of the tiger but never saw it. They figured that their buddy smelled so bad that the tiger left to find something a bit more civil.

"I have a lot more short bits like that," he said as he walked to the door and probably out of my life. I will regret if I never see him again. We are brothers who served together yet apart. We honor each other with our lives. And that is enough!

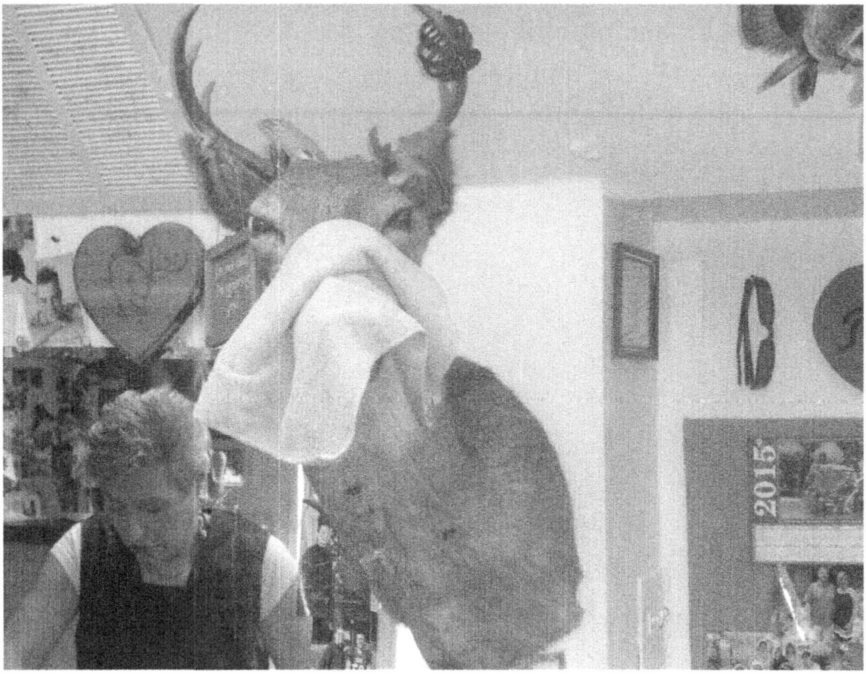
2015

Chapter 20

The Adoption

I am not one of the 'regulars' at the barbershop so I don't know all the people who come in for haircuts, but then again even if I was a regular weekly or two weekly guy, that means I only get a glimpse of the few people already there when I enter or the ones that show up just after I enter. That puts a limit on whom I might see. So it is not too amazing that yesterday as I decided to get a trim that I entered and witnessed two persons of the female persuasion in the establishment and they were not the barbers! One was already in a chair getting a 'Do', let's face it men get haircuts and ladies get 'Dos'. The other was sitting and waiting for a particular barber to have the vacated chair. So I got the empty chair where one lady was getting rearranged.

I sat and glanced at the newspaper a bit while I waited. The day before was election day and the headline was the news that some political party seemed to have bashed the other party pretty hard this time around. That is not too newsy per se since I think that this tends to happen every six years. I would think that in America we are 'Free', free to be fickle and vote our short term feelings not really knowing what direction the country should be going and, therefore, without a clue how to get there. I am not a political person and I have nothing more to say on this topic. I was reading the news, waiting for my turn to have someone with sharp instruments in hand to play around my head and throat. Good thing it was not Halloween and the girl did not have on a mask of sorts!

To tell you the truth I came to the barbershop to listen to a story or two so I could write this story and another in an effort to finish my book (that hopefully you are now reading) before Christmas. I have been working on this for a while, but my habit of not getting the hair cut too frequently seems to have slowed down the progress. But here I am and I got two thoughts as I waited my turn.

A grandmotherly lady was getting her 'Do' and talking about getting ready to meet family who were in China working out the last steps of an adoption of a child. Not being too much of an expert on this kind of thing I first let my mind wander back to the days when in America there were such things as Orphanages filled with children who were orphaned or abandoned. You don't really hear about orphanages in America anymore. Oh, once in a while you might hear about a child put in protective custody or a foster home, but not into an orphanage. And I know from talking to a few people who had adopted children from other countries that they could not find a child in America. The lines are too long and not many children come up for adoption. So off people will go to other countries for the chance of obtaining a child in need of a good home and the safety and comfort that can be afforded.

I know of three families who adopted children. I am not going to use names, but I would like to use the countries without knowing all of the details of the process. The first couple obtained their two children, one at a time, from Korea. They worked out the details to adopt a girl and then a boy. That adoption happened years ago before I met this couple. I can remember talking to the man and he said something about his child over in some part of a building.

The New Book

When I looked I saw three children and I knew two of them but not the third. I got to thinking I was missing something since I saw an oriental type face. I stayed quiet not wanting to feel dumb or ignorant. It turned out I was pretty ignorant since I had no idea the couple had adopted. Later when I got my act together I would tell the father that the boy looked almost exactly like him! We would both get a good laugh and go on with other topics.

The second couple adopted two children from Russia. The children were moderately dark skinned and were actually from one of the far flung parts of the old Soviet Union. Again there were a boy and a girl and they were nice and comfortable to have as part of my community. I would do what I could to get to know these children since they were young and lived close by.

I can remember the trials of the parents as they traveled to Russia to get the children and go through the process to adopt and bring the children home. It would seem that a country that is allowing children to be adopted would make it easy to clear the children, but it seems that the process is tedious. I trust that is because Mother Russia wants only the best for the fruit of her loins! Again I am a bit ignorant on this topic. I just know that there seemed to be a struggle to get everything together for the transfer. Now several years have passed and the children are just a joy to know. A loving couple has taught the children how to love and feel safe and wanted.

The third party is a remote family of the Ehorn clan. They adopted two Chinese Girls over the years and I can see in the photographs how happy both the parents and the children are. I have never met this family but I know of them from a circumstance that I think is a bit bazaar. The man shares my name and my birth date (but not the year, he is younger, I am more handsome).

Any of these three parties could tell similar stories about obtaining the children and traveling to the countries to pick up the children. In every case the parties had to make at least two trips to get the task completed. But it seems that all have been satisfied with the results and are truly raising the precious children as if they were biological family.

So there I was faking reading the Chicago Tribune with the polls almost completed and listening to a grandmother tell the story of her daughter and son-in-law now in Hong Kong completing the process to bring home a boy child. There was a certain amount of pride in grandma as she told her story. The boy was full of joy and had not one ounce of fear in this new adventure he was going to take. Not knowing the people who were going to carry him home to America on his 'first' airplane flight was going to be a real experience. Grandma could hardly wait to welcome the child into the family. There was genuineness in her voice that seemed to show her inner feelings of this event now in the making.

I would have liked to hear more of the story, but I could not get all of the conversation as a few people came into the shop and moved about. Then the conversation in the other chair was underway and took of some of the bandwidth that my ears could use in such times.

Don'tcha just love it when you hear such stories and know that there are loving couples out there who are willing to take in a 'stranger' and make this person part of the family – forever!

This is what America is all about. A couple is just a small part of the symbol of how the country came together. People came to this land and were taken in and the masses of people found a place for the new arrivals and for the most part we have all lived in some sort of harmony. Let's stay focused on the larger picture and not some of the small bad examples. The Lady of the Harbor is still welcoming new people this day. Keep your hearts open to give a hand to the few and the many.

I think Winfield is doing its part!

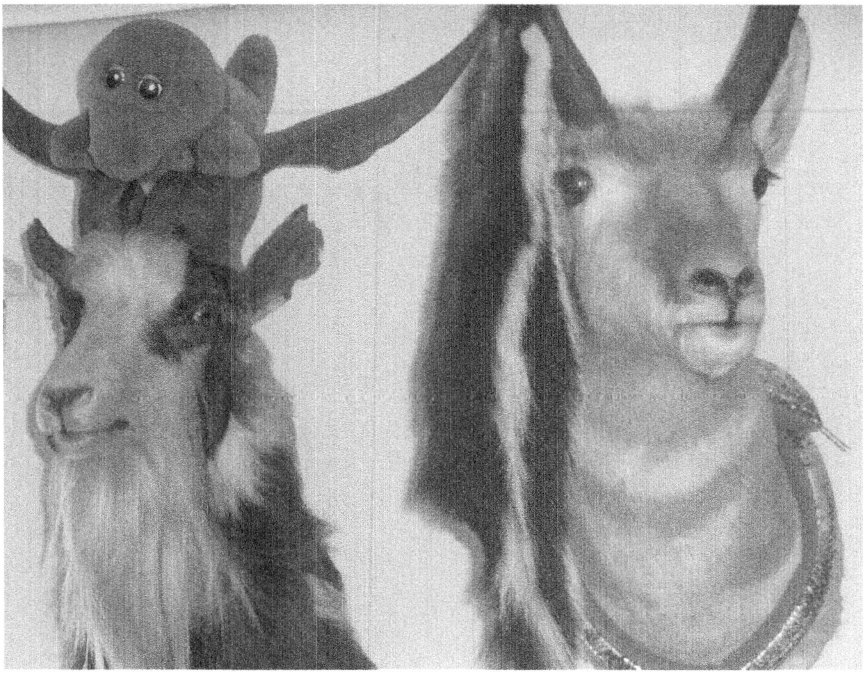

Chapter 21

Between the Holidays

I am not so sure that this is a good name for this piece. Is Halloween a holiday? Certainly Thanksgiving is. It may not make too much difference in the long run. America is now in between the two holidays and just coming down from the longtime of nightly calls from people we hardly know who want our vote. I will now ignore that part of this season.

It is November 5 and the temperatures of any given day start at about 40 and rise as high as 63 or so. With partly cloudy skies and the silver rays of sunlight falling from the heavens above one can get into a fairly good mood and want to take that last stroll before the weather finally turns and makes one put on a heavy sweater and a coat for that walk. Cold fronts move in and blow over the lake bringing gusts of wind that blow my neighbors leaves onto my property. Last year I told Butch that I was going to write his name on every leave of the maple tree at the edge of his property so he would be reminded to clean up after his tree. I can assure you that it didn't work. So I go on my rider mower and cut the leaves into little pieces. So now a yellow haze exists in my side yard until the next rain falls and makes these particles seem to disappear. Where do these pieces go?

Anyway, on this day at the barbershop I sat waiting my turn. I was going to be next up in one of the two active chairs today. Two chairs were not working. Management seemed to know that Wednesday afternoons were not too busy and so only two barbers were needed. People would not mind too much waiting their turns.

These days waiting a turn is not like in the early 1900s. The barbershop has taken a turn in the societal importance of the community. In the early days, men would come to the shop just to sit and talk about what was going on in the community or the country. It was a place to exchange ideas and thoughts about how things were going. Checkers and other things were going on in area that was established just for that purpose. Nowadays, people are more in a rush to get their hair cut and get on their way. As I sat waiting my turn a few men would stop in, take and look and say to one of the girls, "I'll be back later." In America in this day and age, we are in a hurry to get to someplace for some time so we can wait in another place or at least spend our time moving about from place to place where things are busy and you might want to spend time moving to another location using the same 25 minutes to drive instead of just waiting.

Curious?

So the man in chair two is relaxed and getting his share of attention. The gal cutting his hair is adept in pushing the conversation along so that the man will not really get too bored and wonder when this trim will end. As I sit in the chair waiting and watching I see the adept hands of the gal move about working the greying hair as she asks questions and probed life. She might be writing her memoirs and filling it in with some stories that she had coaxed out of a customer. Or perhaps if she entertained the man long enough she would get a bit better tip. I am not the judge and I know not the financial end of the transaction.

The New Book

"So, what are you going to do for Thanksgiving?"

I really don't know; you'll have to ask the boss!"

This is typical of men in this environment. They have no clue as to what is ahead, except the football game and a crowd so large that the wife will pester him if he falls asleep with the grandchildren around the house.

Some conversation will go on with the gal talking about Thanksgiving at her house and all of the kids in and about. Mom and dad will make it one more time to the festivities. You have to make sure this occurs since time is rushing forward all too fast and closing some of the human accounts with each passing month. The season is a mix of fun and celebration along with cold weather and bluster of the wind. The conversation at Thanksgiving is about what to do for Christmas. Always one holiday ahead, the discussions are aimed at what might be next instead of focusing on the here and now.

"Aunt Em is coming from Iowa and Uncle Henry might not come since he is scheduled to break his leg a week from now!"

There is always something about in the room of many conversations. While in the barber chair one can only conjure these thoughts up and allow them to float around filling in time.

"Oops! I took off a bit too much here. I guess I will just start all over!"

So how did Halloween go?"

"I had a hundred kids!"

"Curious, I had none!"

While I did not want to enter the conversation I thought. 'I had only nine.' I was prepared this year to give only full sized candy bars, not those little things you tend to get. Mr. Stingy only gave you one of those small things. The guy next door gives you three and sometimes he makes a mistake and gives you four. I might go change my costume and come back again.

Wasn't it cold and blustery that night? Yes it was and some rain. It kept the kids at home. So why did you get one hundred?

Don't rightly know.

Life tends to go on and the conversations will continue no matter who is in the chair.

Today I had a short wait to get my hair cut. I was looking for at least two stories that I could use in my book. I got them and now I could relax and just think about weird stuff like, 'What are there four different types of barber chairs here?' I am going to have to research that thought when I have time. I guess not everything is spontaneous.

Chapter 22

Cytoplasm – a remembrance

"Step right up kid. The cost of this ride is a mere farkle. Yes, you heard it right – one small, copper farkle. It is the cost of half of an orcMon."

When Tommy heard that, he got excited and put his hands in his pocket to see if he still had one farkle left over.

"You'll not regret this, son. This will be the ride of your life," said the hawker as he took the squared coin from the boy. He bite the coin to make sure it was not a sugar substitute and then opened the gate to the ride.

Without any indication that there was a door in front of him, the boy stood for a moment wondering what he was going to do. Then as if by magic or suggestion, a door slide sideways up into a corner of the building. A sound that the boy never heard before came roaring out at him. Jumping back to get out of the way of a lion or a tiger, the boy stumbled on a stack of posters.

"What are these?" he said. Picking one up, he read the paper.

Here is the most fantastic ride that was ever put together! You spin and whirl seemingly out of control. You build and break

down and then become transformed from one thing to another. You are now on the wondrous Krebs Cycle. Sit back and enjoy. This ride is interactive, so be prepared to participate.

"Whoa! This is too much."

With that said, Tommy got on the ride and sat in a middle car so he would not get too splashed if the ride went down a big slide and plunged into water. No sooner had he buckled himself in, the ride started. A large door opened in front of him and there was a mouth large enough to swallow him and the car he was in.

The car paused and a sign with two buttons came down from above.

"You have to make a choice," the sign read. "Push one of the buttons in front of you in the car."

Tommy looked down. Those buttons were not there when he sat down. How did that happen?

"This is going to be a wild ride," he thought.

So he looked back at the sign. It had changed so that Tommy would know which button to push.

Push the red button if you want to go to <u>eukaryotic</u> side of life. Push the blue button if you might prefer the prokaryotic side.

Tommy had no idea what this all meant, but instinctively he pushed the red button since it was the first choice. Life is that way. Have you gone to a polling place and taken a ballot and finally found out you don't know anyone. You mark the first people on the ballot and finish voting. Most politians know that and they get their petitions in as soon as possible to get first on the ballot. Tommy would learn this in another twenty years. But that is another story.

The New Book

His finger pushed hard on the red button. The car automatically veered left and into a tunnel that looked like an esophagus. It passed the tonsils and was on a descending track. Sure enough there was a large splash as the car fell into a large area that was the interior of a stomach. The stuff that splashed was not water. It was gooey and had slime.

Being a boy, Tommy yelled with joy. He watched as his body started to come apart.

A speaker came on and said, "Don't worry about be broken down. In the end you will be transformed into something wonderful."

So Tommy watched as his arms became soft and squishy. One of them sort of melted and was gone. Tommy had no feelings about any of this. He just watched at this point.

The voice said:

In eukaryotic cells, the *cytoplasm* is that part of the cell between the cell membrane and the nuclear envelope. It is the jelly-like substance in a cell that contains the cytosol, organelles, and inclusions, but not including the nucleus. In fact, the cytoplasm and the nucleus make up the protoplasm of a eukaryotic cell.

In prokaryotic cells that do not have a well-defined nucleus, the *cytoplasm* is simply everything enclosed by the cell membrane. It therefore contains the cytosol, and all the other cellular components, including the chromosome in the nucleoid region.

Supplement

The cytoplasm (of both <u>eukaryotes</u> and <u>prokaryotes</u>) is where the functions for cell expansion, <u>growth</u>, <u>metabolism</u>, and <u>replication</u> are carried out.

Now all of that is very interesting if you are into biological functions other than potty training. However, the information is most irrelevant to most people walking the streets of New York. They could care less that they are a walking manufacturing warehouse with those small little ATPs breaking down to ADP + a phosphorous ion with the break down releasing heat.

Tommy would soon know that he was going to become cytoplasm. He was going to put on a little hard hat to protect his head and thoughts while he continued the ride in the slime of life. He could feel the heat of the ATP breakdown. It warmed him for a while. Then he moved on into a body cell. The conditions there were cool and there seemed to be a constant movement in some swirling motion. Little things floated by as Tommy tried to become adjusted to his condition.

Life in a cell! Wow! Tommy jumped on an organelle and rode around looking at everything. He came up against the nucleus and stopped the ride so he could see what was inside that smaller package. The dark walls were like that screening that people put on the windows of their cars so no one can look in.

Reaching out, he touched the membrane. It was soft and pliant. It sprang back into shape when he withdrew his finger.

A voice called out, "Don't do that again. You might cause a mutation of the DNA."

Tommy gave it some thought. If the DNA mutated, his end would be different. But how would he really know since he had

The New Book

never taken this ride before. For a few minutes he rode around the cell. He pulled some levers and pushed some buttons and everything seemed to be working alright no matter what he pushed. He sat on another organelle for a few moments and watched the cell he was in expand and grow.

Within a few minutes five ATP molecules lined up at some imaginary line and started to run down an unseen track. Each in its turn released a phosphorus ion and let off some steam – heat -you might call it. Now the cell was growing using the internal heat to power the growth. The quick growth pushed Tommy off his organelle and he was swimming around in the fluids of life.

As he floated along the inclusions were like clouds. He watched as they changed shapes. There was one that looked like a clown, another like a lion, another like an angel, as the fluids pushed them along they continued to morph to new shapes that Tommy could not name.

He was finally slowed down by the reticulum and he could reach another organelle and take a seat once again.

Along came a cleaner truck and found Tommy and thought he was not part of the cell and like a computer removing malware, the cleaner swooped Tommy up and carried him away.

In some dark recess of the body Tommy was sliding down a tube like he was at a water park. Just when he could see some light up ahead, he realized that he was tired.

In fact he was pooped!

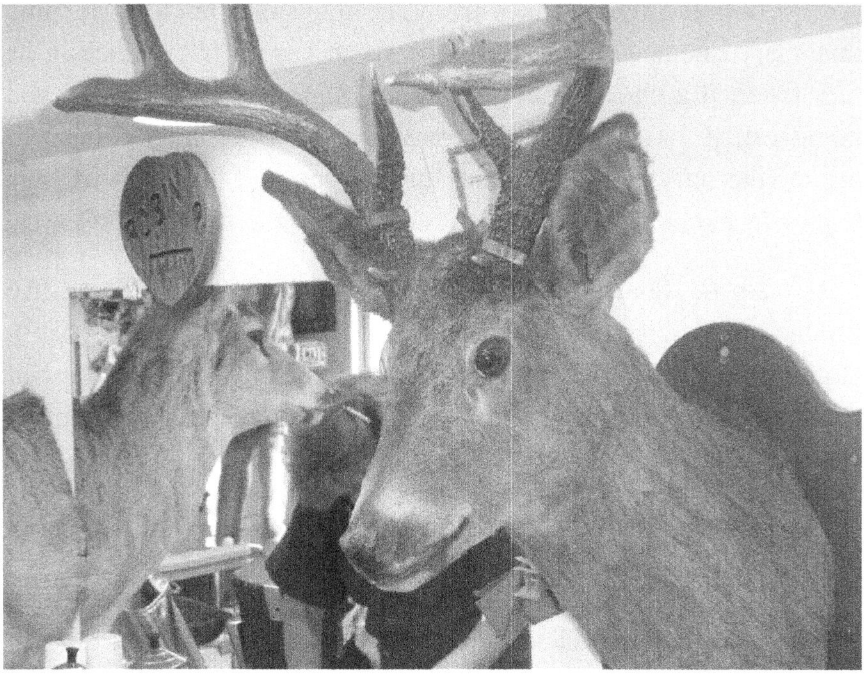

Chapter 23

Checkers at the Barber Shop

For more than five months it seemed that the only contact that had made any difference at all was the two hours that Hal spent playing checkers with that man in the rags. Both of the men sat in the shade during the hottest part of the day in front of the barber shop trying to avoid as much of the sunlight as possible. Hal would bring his checker board to the village square each morning and look for someone to play with. He had more than one person who would spend some time. But for many days it seemed that the old man in rags got to the square first and was sitting by the southern building where he knew there would be shade within the next hour.

The table for the game was a log from an acacia tree that was about 22 inches high. It was somewhat of a miracle that it had not been chopped up for fire wood. This log was a valuable thing to those who had to scrounge for wood each day for the cooking stove. In the village it was rare that you might be able to convince enough people to leave this log so that Hal could come and use it for games. Enough of the men had been interested enough in either playing or watching that the log was simply set off limits for chopping.

By nine thirty each day, the chores in the homes were completed and there was rarely any other work to do, at least for the men. The women had to wash clothes and care for infants and cook. They did these tasks with a joy that most westerners might not understand. The women sang and wandered about in what might look like disarray but they had method in each step they took. In Africa, you did not want to waste too much energy. The sun punished those who were foolish. The women paced themselves and the men stood around in shady spots and watched the village and any action such as the checker match.

Hal had tried for months to get one or two of the village men to come and talk to him. On a straight one-on-one basis it was impossible. No one wanted to just sit and talk. The men wanted some type of action that kept them in the shade but kept their minds in action. Lazy eyes would seem to roll in the heads of the men as they stood watching each move of a piece on the checker board. Hal had learned that he had to play in such a way that the men in the village could win games so that they would return each day. If he won always the men would go find something they could do without him. On the other hand, there were a couple of men who understood the game well and Hal could not beat them, at least not very often.

The smiles on the faces of the men would grow and shrink as the game would proceed. The area was never quiet, but sometime the volume of the voices was great with excitement. Some men would have little side bets going about the outcome of the game. A few would even take bets about what the next move might be.

Hal would get the game going and then he would sort of talk to himself and perhaps even pray about some thing or event. The men would hear the words, but most let the talk pass without any thought or comment. They simply were there to watch the game and pass time. But the words even if they seemed to fall on deaf ears might take root some day in the future. That was about all Hal could hope for on some occasions.

In the afternoons, Hal and his wife would go to market and buy local produce. They tried to grow a few things in their fenced in yard, but the weather was tough in the village area where little shade was about. Water had to be carried from a stream at least a half mile from the village. Hal had paid two men to carry water for the house. They did a good job and seemed faithful enough. Money seemed to speak to these men a bit. Money could be used in many ways. It also attracted the worst sorts of people. You could not have much money in your house or some stealy boy might break in and rob you. Local gangs did roam the area and send the youngest boys they could control to steal from people from time to time.

Suzie had a house keeper who would try to keep the house clean. The sand from the desert seemed to blow everywhere and find a way into houses even when you thought the windows and doors were well closed. Fine dust seemed to cover everything by mid-morning. The cleaner would wipe the dust away and then come back in three hours and do it again.

Tonight Suzie was going to cook a portion of that rabbit she bought in the market place yesterday. Cutting it in half, she put it into a pot with some filtered water and began to stew the rabbit. Turnips and greens would be added later along with some local spices that were difficult to spell or even say. So I am just going to say spices and let you imagine what you will. At the end a carrot was placed in the pot to add some color. The housekeeper had a small fire pit outside the house and would cook flat breads every other day. The bread could be dipped into the stew to assure that it was edible and soft. One day in the hot sum drew all of the moisture out of the bread and left something that was more like crust than bread.

Last week Hal had asked the men in the game circle if they would come and help with a few chores at the church compound. Most of course would not. But three men said they would help just as soon as the sun was setting. They would have about two hours of time they might give. In return for help, the men would get some small bags of salt and sugar. These items were hard to get in the back areas of Mali. It was somewhat of a conundrum that more of the men did not come and help to get the items, but in some ways many men did not want to have someone say that they were becoming Christians, even if all they did was offer physical labor.

Life in the village was ancient and most men were not going to move very much in any mental way. Hal and Suzie would talk to men and women during the day as they played games, purchased goods, held small parties and held church services. The talk and singing in the village gave the people something to hear and think about. Hall knew that all the growth had to come from God. He was told to be faithful and stay on target. Get out there and interface with the people. If one man or woman finally came to know Jesus as savior, perhaps a whole family might see the light. So life went on for years as the two were faithful to their call. Who can judge what God has in store?

In the meantime, Hal would go about losing a few more games to keep the men interested.

There is a parable here somewhere that needs to be written. Simple things in simple places to those who need to be reached. What say you?

Chapter 24

Broken Water and other things

I like to feel miserable. I guess that is about as good as it gets on some days. I try to find things that make me mad, but it is getting tougher or maybe I am just adjusting to the new newness that seems so new! So what is a fella to do?

I took up a hobby to see if I could empty the time that has been stored in the jar on the back shelf for most of the year. My brother gave me that 'Time Capsule' as he called it and said I could either breathe it in or waste the time inside. I think I might just waste it since I am not so sure what one serves with stale air that is time marked. If you have a recipe, please let me know.

Anyway, I took the jar with me and asked a banker if I could make a deposit for the past. He looked a bit confused until I showed him the 'Time Capsule.' Then he seemed to understand.

"Can you wait her just a minute," he said and walked away. The next thing I know the bank was closing for the day. I had three cobwebs on my arms from waiting so long. I think I entered the bank in February and here it was half past June.

Being hungry I went to the soup kitchen and had a roast beef sandwich. The liquid kind of course. I had a bit of trouble holding the bread together. Even the stale bread seemed too wilted to be used appropriately. I made a mess of the ceiling as the dripping were falling upward as if some force from outer space was redirecting the droplets of the green colored stuff. I called it stuff since the guy with the ladle called it a dirty word that my mom won't let me say. If I make it to fifty-five and I going to go into the church next door and shout it out. Won't everyone be surprised that I had yelled out, "Bad Words!" I will just run away then and I will not turn back like those two girls in the Bible did. Not that salt is such a bad thing, but too much of it ... I well I guess I really don't know how to end that paragraph. Let's try a new one.

In the Big Innings, sort of like the third quarter of the Hockey Match, I knew just what to do. I was given the wicket and I charged ahead and let fly with the ointment of life. Everyone scattered and I slide home. The Pastor called me, "OUT!"

Guess he was the one in the church that day!

Anyway, I was trying to say that I liked to break water. You have to sneak up on it from the front and put a hold on the trickle gizmo. If you hold it tight it will spray you with a power that is most annoying. Next you take a piece of string and bind it to your finger to remind you of what you are about to do. In the future when I first did this, I had red string. I can tell you now red just doesn't work. You can't get any traction. Water is slippery until you tie it down. Blue thread works well, but perhaps green would be okay.

I broke my first water as a baby, I am told. I don't think I want to give that sentence much more thought. The red thoughts I might have had at that point would never get out of my mind if I let them in. I morphed just after I was born. Mom said I was cute. My dad slapped my mother and asked, "What the Hell is this?"

But that is another story.

The New Book

Water is broken best on Thursdays after a strong wind clears the table inside the hotel room you rented. With the blue string attached you simply ... wait a second I have to check this out before I write it ... a ten minute break is now authorized ... hum di dum di dum.

It is now okay to proceed with lies and tall stories.

The water got out of hand, slippery little fellow that it was. I felt my hands dry as if the desert wind was taking away my moisture to feed it to the White Rabbit. Was it Alice or was it Jefferson Airplane? Don't recall at this point. The water was walking toward the door officer. I felt threatened so I just shot it like a coyote which had rabies or mental illness.

I know now that you think this is nonsense, but if you read every other word backward, you will find my special message. Contact me a Winkum Blinkum and Nod. Our offices are on the water front as you might expect.

I see the word count is up to eight hundred thirty-nine, opps, if I type more then the count goes on. How do I end this with a word count of nine hundred? Only thirty-seven more words to go.

Four score and eight years ago was 1926.

I like the men in the white coats. They are coming to take me back in. So I will say good bye.

It must be time for my nearly annual haircut. I will rob the piggy bank and head over the see the gals. Will they remember me?

Is it any wonder that the men seem to crowd round and try their hand at playing checkers and Wort? I think not, but then under the influence of Blue Moon who would know for sure.

Oh, I'm sorry some of you don't know about wort, do you? Wort is the early part of beer in both beer brewing and whisky making. It tastes awful, perhaps!

I broke some water with the ninth golf ball that went into the ponds at Arrowhead. I could earn a lot of money diving for these spheres.

Do the gals cut hair under water? Just ask them.

It is time to stop all of this fun and try to make a book of it!

Have fun now.

Chapter 25

The Not So Silent BarberShop

Ding ding ding

Creak, creak, clunk

Snip, snip snip

Buzz, buzz

Thunk, thunk

Squir-rr-r-t, fizz

Whirl, whirl

Slip, slide, slip

Buzz, whirl, whiz

Scrap, scrap

Ding, ca-ching

Rupple, pop, rupple, crackle

Slip, slide, slip

Murmur, murmur, buzz, snip, snip, Bzz

Thunk, thunk

Slip, slide

Ding, ding

Next!

Chapter 26

Moving the Heads About

It happens I guess. Every business will finally come to an end, or at least it will change hands and then when you move out of town you will not know if it ever closed or not. So I am going to take the position that sooner or later everything will close down. I have seen this occur in the past six years with many businesses that could not make it through the last dire financial times. People are out of work, looking for work and underemployed. Others are just hitting those magic years when it is time to close the doors on their professional lives and find some rest in other activities that don't create schedules, well not totally since there are schedules for a lot that don't include work!

Robin, the owner of Sportsmans Barber Shop, has recently commented that she was contacted by a couple in West Chicago who have owned and operated a barbershop for over thirty years. For any number of reasons it was time to stop. Now there are a couple of options that might be associated with this decision.

First, you can just tell everyone who has frequented the shop that they will just have to let their hair grow long since the barbershop will be closed before there is a need for the next cut.

Personally I like this option since I am one of those who too infrequently gets my hair cut and if Robin were a man she would grow a long beard before I made my return to the chair. I am sure that is not a good option for many of the people who will find the lights out on their return trip to their favorite place. So I guess we must look at option two.

The second option is to try to let everyone know that with the closing of a shop that there is a good alternative. And that is just what the couple in West Chicago did. They first made a contact to Robin and told her that they were closing down. Then they told her that they would like to refer the clients to the Sportsmans for future cuts. Robin was pleased with the decision.

As we sat in the barber chair yesterday Robin talked about this matter as a response to my probing about some new item that could be used as a story. I am not sure that she thought this would end up in the book and after reading this you might think she was on to something. Anyway in the casual time between haircuts when there were no new clients around, Robin relaxed in her chair and just let the thought flow. You could feel her emotion about having new clients coming her way.

"I took some of my business cards over to the shop so they could be handed out!"

I guess that would be a pretty good indication that she thought that the new clients would be great. Then she said, "The people over there will fit in nicely with the ones we already have, they are mostly retired people!"

I looked up from my chair – I was done with my hair cut and just hanging around – you know in those kinds of times without a mirror in front of me I feel like I am 35 years old and not double that. I was feeling for a few seconds that I was now in a group of old codgers who used canes to get to the water stations that we need for both ends of our bodies. But instead of asking for my cane, I decided to be polite and just ride the discussion out.

"Well, I am glad to hear that you will be increasing your customer base," I lied. "Having more customers is a real asset to you and the other gals here."

I think one of the reasons I like the barbershop here is that you normally don't have to wait more than five minutes to get into the chair. I am both patient and impatient and I cannot control those sides of me, ask my wife! I think back over the years and I know that I got to not getting haircuts since it was a waste of time, sitting too long, and a waste of money, the hair just grew back anyway.

Now my attitude has changed. I like going to the barbershop as often as I think about it, a lot of times not often enough. It is a place to listen to and share stories.

So with a whole new set of people who might come through the door I can get excited about what they might bring with them. I will look forward to a West Chicago story and a few comments about how this shop compares with the old shop.

All I can say is this ... We in Winfield are a lucky group to have such nice gals cutting our hair! I have never been disappointed. I like to respond some times when I am out of control that I want my hair cut longer. I get a little kick in the ... dark ... and then I finally say, "The Usual." It is nice being known at the barbershop.

Now the question is – When will they put out a table so we can play checkers?

A Tribute to Marthe Raye
Colonel U.S. Army

May her life as a soldier be remembered as well as all the other Veterans from Winfield.

Chapter 27

Cantigny Revisited

With all the hope that Robert McCormick intended as he built his home in DuPage County years ago, he had a plan that included not only the time of his life, but would extend into the future for thousands of folks to enjoy. I am sure that he would take great pleasure in seeing and hearing the crowds come through the grounds to see what is growing and find a bit of the child within. In the vast array of planted materials is a veritable treasure trove of color and fragrances that stir the inner mind and heart making them fly on magic carpets to imaginary places where some joy is allowed to enter.

No matter who you are and what you might be seeking on any given day when you enter the grounds, you will be met with more stimulation than you might have thought possible even if you have been in this place before. The rich tapestry of the grounds is made of threads of native trees mixed in with shrubs and flowers, richly planted in large groves that make your eyes weary as they move around to try to make some personal sense of all that is encountered. The eye flashes from side to side, the pupils see yellows, reds, oranges, green, and blues in hues and shapes that tantalize.

If you allow yourself to dream, you will see the tree nymphs and elves dancing around and Pan plays the flute with some ancient tune that was written by the gods. A unicorn pulls a wagon of children to a place where trees grow sugar plums and sweet morsels that never grow stale.

Moms and Pops, too, find warmth and comfort in this place where the rainbow has more than once set its pot of gold amongst the flower gardens insisting that each flower stand tall for the visitors until relieved of duty. For this is the place of the Big Red One and it is Duty, Honor and Country for everything and everyone who might call this place home.

In the still of the night the fairies can be seen dancing around as they take a palate of paint and redecorate the flower garden. Splashes of vibrant color fly everywhere and enhance a plant that might have grown a bit weary in the sun. The elves bring their small buckets of water and pass them hand to hand from the pond to the flower beds to refresh the soil and stimulate growth and vitality. When the dawn arrives, tired little bodies will soon retreat to their holes in the ground or in a pleasant tree and all will seem to be ready for the children to find their fun. Laughter will fill the air and bring joy to the workers now trying to sleep, but having one ear attuned to the sounds so they know just where they will need to focus the next night's work. For no small corner can be allowed to sag and be seen as unattended.

The garden is a community and it all works together to bring its pride to the folks who would care to walk the grounds. In some places you can see that the flowers are having a fashion show to display their finery and flirt with passersby. Each season has its own select areas that bring a focus and a new adventure. Pansies, and petunias waltz with the marigolds with the background of the boxwoods being their green screen.

If some of this does not grab your heart and you need another outlet for your soul, the museum may provide you with a reason to

The New Book

come and learn about those who knew that freedom had a cost and they were willing to pay the entry fee. Some paid it all.

With movies and exhibits and two bunkers one from WW1 and one from WW 2, the place was an adventure land for me in my youth. I could role play and pretend for a few hours that I was engaged in the Battle for Cantigny or the Battle of the Bulge knowing in advance that I was going to live through these battles and walk out the door at the end of the role play. In my mind all was going to be well. How would I ever know how horrible the days were if you were at the original battlefields? Terror beyond belief would fill your heart and your soul would find no rest in the muddy trench that was going to save your life for a while. Tomorrow would be a different day and perhaps you would be ordered over the top by someone way behind the lines. Certainly Generals were selected from the ranks of those men who had no fear of putting their men in harm's way. It might give you pause to think that but then how does one deal with the jubilant men who after the battle is over they rise up and praise the General for pulling them through this adventure.

After I went to war I still could not find within myself that glue that made one rise up and run face long into machine gun fire. I did have a new respect for some of those who did, but not all. Some I fear are just crazy and could care less about what comes next. How do you respect that type? Others seem to understand that life could end in the foxhole or on the field. God had already made an entry in the book of life about when. You just are required to show up at the spot at the time written. Makes little sense I am sure.

The beaches of Normandy spoke to me as I stood on the cliff and wondered what drove men up the cliffs. I will never recover from that moment of truth. The time gave birth to feelings I had inside me and made me a part of the Band of Brothers.

I had been in the war zone and heard the noises of the rockets and bombs. I saw the pock marks of the bombs. I felt the fear as I lay in a trench along an airstrip in the middle of the night wondering how this all happened to me. Now I stand when called upon as people remember that I served. But in my heart I know I had the easy part and I hoped I did a good enough job to save a few men on the ground.

Now I come to Cantigny to hear concerts. I am allowed free access since I served. This may seem like little compensation for time spent on the line in Viet Nam, but I am thankful for the small remembrance as I place my folding chair in front of the bandstand with many other grey-hairs who also served their time. We are united one more time and I am proud that I am amongst the best of the best.

What does Cantigny mean to me? It is a place where I am allowed to be free to remember the good and the bad of the times when politians cannot seem to communicate enough to avoid the horrors that they will not attend personally. It is a place to gather for many reasons. It is a place that allows celebration that includes our heroes. It is a place where I can get lost in the flower gardens when the memories of the past battles become too much. Colonel McCormick knew we would need this place. So he set aside an estate and played fox and hound, planted the garden and dreamed big dreams. Now he has allowed the veterans to enjoy a part of his life.

Here was a man who did not have to go to war, but choose to go and then remembered those who marched with him. Thank you Robert!

Chapter 28

The Garden

As I entered the barbershop there was one guy who was getting out of the barber chair and paying for his cut. The two other girls, both named Robin, were sitting in the window seats since no one was waiting for a cut.

"Do I have to take a number?"

"We don't do that here."

"So who is going to get to cut my hair?"

"We have a rotation here and it is my turn."

"Well, that is nice. I enjoy how you cut my hair so I am sure we will have a good time."

I started the 'chair' conversation that morning.

"I remember last time I was here you talked about making the cucumber salad."

"Oh, I think you mean the cucumber salsa. Yeah, I made it and it was delicious. I got the recipe off the internet. It was the second recipe listed when you log in. It is the one that uses lime juice."

I was thinking that there are always changes in the listing on the net so the recipe she talked about might not be in the same rotation. "I'll give that a look when I get home!"

"Yeah I made it since last year's garden was so plentiful. I had way too many cucumbers and I was looking for things to do with them. I think I made five or six batches."

"Sounds good."

"Do you have a garden?" she asked.

"No, I only tried to raise a few tomatoes in the back yard in the few sunny spots that I have that might support a garden. There are far too many trees in the back to support a garden."

"I have had a garden for about six years. Most years the garden is pretty good and I get a lot of vegetables. Last year the peppers and tomatoes did not do so well. I tried the regular tomatoes and they were poor. The small ones, I think they call them 'grape tomatoes' did pretty well."

"A number of people I know said that the tomatoes and peppers last year did not produce very well. I have heard any number of things from poor seeds to weather conditions. I would bet that the cool weather in the spring and lower temperatures in the summer had a lot to do with the peppers. I think they need hot days!" I said.

"That could be. I will try to raise them again this year. Last year I got the tomatoes from Ace Hardware and the other plants for a nursery. I wonder if that had anything to do with the production."

"I would think that is hard to say for sure. But you might look for some slightly bigger plants this season and get them in the ground as soon as possible. Do you grow things like broccoli or cauliflower?"

"I haven't done that before. My husband is not too much into the garden. He tells me that it is more difficult to cut the grass around the garden, thus more time is spent. I have told him that it is worth the effort and I guess that he has come to know that the garden is a fact of life and he will just have to deal with it. I like being outside as much as possible and it is a good thing to have time outside doing something productive. "

"Well those are cold weather plants and you can put them in the ground sooner. When the temperature rises you might want to cover the plants with a cheese cloth to keep the direct sun off of them."

"I'll give that some thought to that cheesecloth thing."

I was fairly sure that the broccoli plants would not be purchased or planted. I could careless to tell you the truth.

"I just haven't grown tomatoes in the back for a few years. The amount of sun I get is not conducive to their growth. When the tomatoes come in I get a lot of free ones from friends and I buy a bunch of 'ugly tomatoes' at the markets that are misshaped. You get them half price. I make 'ugly salsa' from them; about 16 to 25 quarts each year. The salsa never seems to make it to the next summer since I give most of it away as gifts for Christmas or some other special occasion."

My hair cut continued with a few other topics, but nothing as long and intriguing as the garden talk. I must have said something about shoveling the Global Warming off my drive the other day and then we both laughed. But that did not provoke any further conversation.

The two Robins sitting in the other chairs were doing a bit of talking while they waited for the door to open once again. Midday Thursday is slow at the barbershop. It is good for the customer who comes in and does not have to wait but can immediately slip into a chair. The girls have their own idea of a good day and a poor day. Thursday is not necessarily a good day and the tips would be lean to say the least.

In the quiet of the morning the sun filtered past the lettering on the south facing window of the shop leaving shadows across the room on the walls and the floor. Robin sat there for a while and then had to adjust herself so that the sun would not be in her eyes. Spots of hair from some previous cuts were lightly 'sprinkled' across the floor. There was no need to sweep too thoroughly yet since the day had hardly begun.

I looked down and saw my own hair lying in wait for the broom. I wanted it to be a dark brown, but once again it was white, mostly. I still have some color in the hair on the back of my head. Soon the chair swiveled around and I was facing a nice looking guy in the mirror. At first I wondered who might have come into the shop. Then I smiled and the man smiled back at me. I was I. The hair cut made me look … well no use getting into that.

"The hair looks fine," I said to my barber. The cover came off of me to indicate that I was now finished, except settling the account. I pay the senior rate these days and sometimes wish that I got a card that would take nine punches and get the tenth cut free. Pulling a twenty from my pocket I handed it to my barber and told her, "Do as you please with this."

Off into the sunshine I went to tackle another small task before I had to go home and start supper for my wife.

"When will it start to warm up?" I said to myself. Pulling my coat around me a bit, I got in the car and out of the wind. "Maybe tomorrow if the weatherman got it right this morning."

How I View Winfield

Chapter 29

Billie

The full moon woke me this morning racing through my western looking window. The shape reminded me of a nice round of Colby cheese that had yet to be cut. The nice mellow yellow somewhat bordering on gold was just enough to make me want to get up and get moving.

My usual routine of getting up and pulling on clothes in the dark was set in motion one leg at a time as I pull on the trousers. I grabbed my shirt I had laid out the night before and started to the door. Everything seemed just fine in the dark shadows of the morning. Down the stairs with a cadence that seemed to me this morning was a bit too militaristic I arrived on the main floor and was going to go to the kitchen to make some coffee. Here is where the reality of the day seemed to be way out of focus. Things were not as they should be.

The kitchen was the kitchen I had over ten years earlier, not the one I had paid tens of thousands of dollars to upgrade just two years ago. The brown cabinets were wrong! I twisted and turned in all directions and closed my eyes a few times, hoping that the motion would bring me back to reality of where I was when I went to sleep. That was not going to happen. Everything and everywhere seemed to be the old items that my family used ten to fifteen year earlier. I could not explain how this was happening.

In times like these you just turn on the radio or the television and find out when and where you are. I was fairly sure I was in my house in Winfield since at least I knew the old kitchen appliances well enough. The key then seemed to be when am I?

"Good morning Chicago. This is Alan Sudsby bringing you the news at five."

Not who I expected to hear in the morning. This was not right even outside of the house. Something had happened to the world. Or something had happened to me.

"The construction on the Dan Ryan is backing up traffic earlier this morning and the commute times into downtown will be over an hour and fifteen minutes. You might want to find an alternative way in."

That is not right. The construction was completed two years ago. I yelled at the radio asking it to tell me what day it was. With no response I ran out on the drive and picked up the morning paper. Forget the headlines. Look at the date.

Friday, November 13, 1999. I gasped. I had gone to sleep on December 12, 2014 and now somehow the clock had been reset to a time fifteen years earlier. I was sort of a Rip Van Winkle in reverse. There was no logic to this. Things like this don't happen. Well maybe they do, but it is always to some other person, not you or me!

I looked at the headlines for some information that might help me solve my dilemma. There I found the clue and maybe the truth.

"Scientists Worry About Y2K!"

That was fifteen years ago alright. Everyone was worried that the world would stop, at least the electronic parts of the world. Maybe the world did stop and rewind and now I was going to have to relive all of those years over again in a new chance to fix my life. If that were true, I paused to think, what would I do differently? I seemed to have all of my faculties about me since I remembered many of the ensuing years after the year 2000. So I was being given a chance to re-do my life and make some fresh happen. What might that me?

If I changed my life, would it impact the lives of others? The thought of that was much more than I wanted to think about. I could cause calamities in people's lives by doing things and going in different directions than I did the first time around. Was I willing to do that, take that chance?

I sat down trying to think about how I used to make coffee. I would see how I felt after some joe slipped down my throat. A sense of wonder and amazement began to come over me.

"What if ..."

Let me see now. In 1999 I had kids living at home. Was I ready for that again? I had not done an assessment on my body to see if my body was the 1999 variety or the 2015 variety. That certainly would make a difference in how I would feel about things and approach life if I really had to live the fifteen years over again. Since I was sure my mind was the 2015 version, I began to think that the body was going to be the old version. Would I dare to look in a mirror and see the white hair? I better have that coffee first. Yes that might help a bit later when I finally could no longer put off the observation.

As the coffee brewed, taking its sweet time I might add, I sat on a chair and was tossing a few thought around in my head. If I am old living in the past, I could make the best of it, couldn't I? I might not be able to move about so freely, but I could compensate by using my noggin to full advantage. The one thing I knew that was helpful was that I knew unless I did something stupid that I would be alive in the year 2015. That took pressure off some things but placed a certain burden on other aspects of life.

"Whew, this is going to be complicated!"

It might be a lot of fun telling those concerned about Y2K that nothing was going to happen. The computers would continue on without a hitch and life would exist on the other side of December 31, 1999. Then I would say something that might have put me in the looney bin, "I was or am there right now!" Knowing I would get strange looks and several people, even those close to me, would wonder if I had lost it under the stress of my job. The other thing I had to consider was if I should tell people about events that were going to happen in the future so that they could be prevented. I could almost stop the airplanes from crashing into the buildings in New York. Couldn't I? The cold chill of that thought ran through me. If I told the FBI who they should monitor and why, they are likely to take me to some place where the lights don't shine and the buses don't run. Ah! I could do it anonymously and start with a few small things that would happen soon so that they knew someone had a handle on the future. I could be the walking Nostradamus who seemed to make predictions. My predictions would come in the near future and not be veiled in some codes that were hard to know or understand. What a thought that was! The rush in my mind was crashing like a twenty foot wave on the north shore of Oahu. I saw the vision of that and heard the roar as if I were on the beach. And then suddenly I was on the beach! How did that happen? I had my coffee cup so I was linked to my home somehow, but I had just traveled four thousand miles in the blink of an eye to hear and see what I thought. Amazing! Terrifying!!!!!!

A little Old Man stepped out of the shadow and said to me, "How do you like this return to your past?" and before I could respond he said, "It is now your presence forever."

The New Book

I was locked in time to my past and I would just have to deal with it once again. As I sat on the beach my wife came over to me and told me that she was feeling very pleased with her wedding anniversary present of this trip to Hawai'i. I gave her a hug and wondered if she too was taking the same trip I was on.

This trip is brought to you by the makers of Ovaltine!

And of course Sportsmans Barbershop!

Be Happy!!!!

Chapter 30

A Close Shave

No one will really believe this story, but I am going to tell you that it is true ... every word of it. So just sit back and give it a read. Then think back to those days of your childhood when you were willing to believe anything told by someone over eleven years old. Those 'adults' as we might have viewed them at the time were so smart that they could answer any and all questions. So now I am only going to try to bring back a few of those magical days as I close up this book.

It was a dark and cloudy early morning and Jackie had been in the barbershop alone for half an hour. She was the set up lady this day, a task that was shared by all on some rotational basis. All of secrets of the shop were lying about on the counters and the floor and had to be put in containers so that things that were private were safe. While that might not seem possible to most since in the open atmosphere of the shop anyone who stayed long enough was bound to hear a few of those secrets. But in the hustle and bustle of the shop during the day most of the talk at one chair or anther seemed to be a bit garbled. Still when things closed down or got slow the gals would exchange stories and the one who came up with the best story could skip a morning clean up!

The broom was working a wonder on the floor and seemed almost to be a hair magnet collecting all of the small bits that might be missed if someone with tired eyes was doing clean up. One of the gals had sleepy eyes, but that is a secret that we are not allowed to talk about. If you stopped by early mornings and saw one gal who was there early more than any other you just might have a clue.

Oh, the sleepy eyes would not really matter when the scissors were going wild and flashing about the head and neck. It is called professionalism. But sweeping the floor is not a part that ever got graded in barber school so one had to do on- the-job training. A shop owner would set a standard and then everyone with the daily job would try to work within that framework.

Well, on this dark and cloudy day before anyone else showed up in came a man wearing a 'Pea Jacket' and a rounded white hat. He looked about and saw the sign that said no smoking so he stepped outside and took his pipe and hit it a few times on the rail so the tobacco would fall out and onto the ground. A bit of a grin came over his face as he re-entered the shop.

"Good morning!" said Jackie "Do you want a haircut?"

The man lifted off his hat and clearly with a bald head he did not need a haircut. Jackie tried not to laugh at her question and the situation, but it is a bit hard not to laugh when you get caught up with this sort of situation.

A gruff look came over the man's face.

"I need me a shave. I've got a date with me sweetie Olive Oyl. Ar. Arg. Arg!"

So he moved on heavy feet across the room and sat in a chair that was offered. Jackie took the cloth that was used to cover people and spread it over the man; it did not cover too much since his arms were enormous. She stepped back and then grabbed a second cloth and used the two to cover the man. It was a good thing that the part of the arms that were so huge were the lower parts or she might not have been able to get close enough to the man to complete his shave.

First a hot towel was put on the man's face. The towel would stay there for five or six minutes to begin the process of making the beard soft so it could easily be cut. The man was silent for the time under the towel but when the towel came off his mouth started in on so many things about boats, the sea, mean men and his wonderful girlfriend whom he had not seen in sixteen years. He was sure that she still loved him.

"She loves me. She wrote that to me ten years ago and last year I sent back a card that said, 'I am glad you do!' Now ain't that sweet of me?"

Jackie began to laugh a bit and stopped the process of shaving since she just might have an accident.

"You are some charmer, mister."

"I knows it darling, and so does my sweetie!"

"I got to go over there real soon so let's just get this stubble off'n my face."

Lather covered the entire head and was so thick at first that Jackie could not seem to find his face. What had she done? Wiping the lather off a bit and then spotting the face beneath, she picked up the razor and moved it over the face. Her left hand seemed to smooth the lather as she went. The right hand held the razor and followed the contours of this man's very rounded face.

In just ten minutes the face was smooth and silky like a baby's bottom.

"How do you like your shave?"

The man moved his hand over his face. The chin was smooth and the man was very pleased. Rushing to get over to his true love's house, he seemed to have left his hat on the hook by the door.

Jackie went back to sweeping the floor as if this man had never showed up. There seemed to be huge piles that just kept falling to the floor around each chair. Soon ten waste baskets were full and ten more would be needed.

Robin came in to the shop about ten minutes later and Jackie was still asleep in her chair. The television was blaring with a Popeye Cartoon. Popeye looked out at Jackie and winked, "See ya for a shave next week, honey!"

From the Author

Each day seems to be an adventure that I must follow. I have lived long enough to know the joy and the disappointments of life. I try to only remember the good parts and the wonderful people. If we would all treat people like the wonders that they are and materials things in the way they should be treated, we would all be happier.

It is interesting that this book about the barbershop has been written because the author does not like to go there.

But the thought of writing this book has encouraged him to go multiple times in a month to collect thoughts for a good story line. Look out Winfield, this could get to be a new model of civility for Doug.

Don't leave your family and friends behind

Lest We Forget!

About The Author

Doug Ehorn claims to have been born 150 years too late. He would rather endure the hardships of the pioneers than the pollution of his generation.

Nothing is what it seems to be so Doug concentrates on the things he sees and worries not about what others finally may think.

Raised next to a marsh, Doug enjoys the solitude of being out with nature and seeing those things that most people only read about.

Residing in Winfield, Illinois with a very supportive wife, he breezes through life these days with the songs that the wind provide. Happy to share his little corner of the world, he offers to you this book.

Doug does not cut his hair as often as he should!

As always, this book is written at Casa Blanca!

Lest We Forget!

Made in the USA
Monee, IL
18 August 2022